Texas Theatre Journal

Volume 16 (Fall, 2019)
Texas Educational Theatre Association

Texas Theatre Journal
Vol. 16, Number 1, 2019
ISBN-13: 9781688041622
Copyright © 2019 by Texas Educational Theatre Association
Shelby-Allison Hibbs; John Michael Sefel, Editors

Texas Theatre Journal invites manuscripts on a variety of topics related to theatre and the performing arts, with emphases on history, practice, criticism, and theory. In addition to full-length articles, TTJ publishes profiles, interviews, book reviews, and performance reviews. The journal is particularly interested in research related to the broad geographical, cultural, and historical notion of Texas. We welcome opportunities to support scholars working in Texas. Published annually by the Texas Educational Theatre Association, our mandate is to feature the work of graduate students whenever possible.

Submissions: We value clear, accessible writing for a general audience of theatre educators, scholars, and practitioners. Preferred articles are typically 4000-6000 words in length. Articles should be submitted via email as Word files, following Chicago Style guidelines with all citations/context notes handled as end notes. Article itself should be a reader's copy without author's name or affiliation; submissions should also include a title page with author(s) and affiliated institutions, and an abstract of 500 words or less. Special consideration is given to articles with subject matter connected with or related to Texas and/or the American Southwest. *Profiles and Interviews*: We publish scholarly profiles and rigorous interviews covering theatre practitioners with a Texas connection. Accompanying photos are preferred (author must secure photo permissions). Article, Profile, and Interview submissions should be e-mailed to TexasTheatreJournal@gmail.com

Additional submission information, including how to submit performance reviews, book reviews, and articles for the Texas Educational Theatre Association Scholar Debut Paper Project may be found on page 119.

Texas Theatre Journal

Published Annually by the Texas Educational Theatre Association

CELJ — The Council of Editors of Learned Journals

PREFACE: A CHANGING OF THE GUARD

In 2005, John Hanners and James E. Lile published the first issue of *Texas Theatre Journal*. When Lile stepped away for other obligations, Hanners continued to edit the publication, carrying on a tradition of excellence that would serve the Texas Educational Theatre Association well for seven years. In 2013, it was Hanners' turn to step away from the journal he created, and the stewardship passed to the capable hands of Baylor University's DeAnna Toten Beard. While working toward my MFA in Waco, DeAnna approached me with an intriguing offer to act as her assistant editor. Anyone who knows DeAnna knows that one doesn't turn down an opportunity to work with her, and so I immediately and gratefully accepted. I assumed it would be a one-year gig while I finished up my graduate work, and then it'd be passed along to some other grad student. I also assumed, as an "assistant," I would primarily be doing low-level citation checks and occasionally fetching coffee. No matter, as I knew it would be an amazing opportunity no matter what the task.

What I did not expect, however, was to be treated as a partner and a full collaborator. We quickly found a groove in which DeAnna headed up working with authors, and I took over the physical creation of the journal itself, from designing covers and formatting the innards to learning more than I ever wanted to know about ISBN and UPC codes. It was hectic, exhausting, and wonderful. As I finished my time at Baylor and prepared to head to more northern pastures, DeAnna offered me the position of Co-Editor, solidifying our collaboration and professional friendship as partners-in-editing-crime, proud to represent *Texas Theatre Journal* at the TETA TheatreFest every year. Each issue, I looked forward to the collaboration with DeAnna as much as I looked forward to creating the journal itself.

That is why—when DeAnna was deservedly named Department Chair at Baylor University and, in turn, felt her new duties necessitated stepping away from *TTJ*—I temporarily wondered whether I could stay myself. I knew I couldn't take on putting the entire journal "solo" without risking my own scholarship and my time with my young children ... but to partner with someone other than DeAnna? I just wasn't sure it could ever be as lovely a working relationship again ... and why stick around for something that would no longer be enjoyable?

The fact that I am writing this preface today is an indication of just how wrong I was. I am proud to welcome Shelby-Allison Hibbs, Clinical Assistant Professor at the University of Texas at Dallas, as the new Co-Editor of *Texas Theatre Journal*. Working on this first volume in this new editorial era of *TTJ* has been nothing short of a delight, and it is my earnest hope that you enjoy the work that's contained within.

Of course, our editing partnership represents only a fraction of the work that goes into each journal. I know we are both grateful that our wonderful review editors, Suzanne Delle and Cason Murphy, have once again brought their excellence to the journal. We are grateful for Rebecca Worley, Jackie Rosenfeld, Eric Skiles, and all their wonderful work with the Scholars' Debut Paper Project. We are so thankful for the TETA board and their continued support of our efforts. We are profoundly grateful to each of the scholars who sent us their articles, reviews, and interviews; there would be no journal without you. Finally, there would be no reason to work on any of this without readers—and so, sincerely, thank you.

In this moment of transition, it's an appropriate time to pay homage to just a few of the many who helped us get where we are today and to push ourselves to continue to build and grow into the future. To our illustrious founder, the late John Hanners; to James E. Lile, to our special volume editor Marion Castleberry, and to DeAnna Toten Beard; to every person who has served on our advisory board or worked as a reader or editor; to every librarian who has stocked the book; to the entirety of the TETA board past and present, and to every scholar who has entrusted their work to our journal—thank you. We sincerely hope you'll continue to be pleased as we enter this new period of *TTJ* leadership.

Texas theatre is alive and well, and it is unquestionably because of its devoted, talented, and loving community of educators. Among all the people this volume thanks, in truth, it is this—our community of dedicated, caffeinated teachers and administrators—which have truly made this publication possible and worthwhile.

JOHN MICHAEL SEFEL
Co-Editor, Texas Theatre Journal

EDITOR'S NOTE

Theatre practice remains in a constant state of reforming and reflecting on itself. What we know for certain today will be challenged tomorrow with cultural evolutions along with new understandings of the past. The course of theatre history is "open ended" and never completely permanent. The following essays in this issue of *Texas Theatre Journal* offer insights into the continuous discovery of educational theatre, performance, and historical inquiry.

First, *TTJ* proudly acknowledges its longstanding home within the Texas Educational Theatre Association (TETA). Once again, we are excited to published the winners of TETA's Debut Papers Project. The first is Amanda Rose Villarreal's "It Happens Here", chronicling am interactive theatre experiment to facilitate public conversations on sexual harassment. Villarreal's essay became a centerpiece for this issue as it experiments with applied theatre in an educational environment to engage a broader student body. Villarreal documents this intervention theatre project to hold informal conversations in open spaces, bringing visibility and peer-to-peer dialogues on this important topic. The other winners of the Debut Papers Project include essays by Margaret A. Boos' "A Woman's Place" and Bruce Turk's "Flips, Quips, and Broken Bits".

The intersection of disability studies and theatre is a subject that has brought numerous discussions about privilege and narrative in theatre practice. Representation and public dialogue concerning actors with disabilities has increased in recent years. Certain milestones have occurred, such as Ali Stroker of the current Broadway revival of *OKLAHOMA!* became the first wheelchair user to win a Tony Award for her performance. In this issue, Nicolas Shannon Savard examines the exchange occurring between the audience and a disabled performer in "Cripped Visuality". In the context of a solo performance, what social narratives does the audience create in their participation watching a disabled solo performer? Savard also examines the nature in which a person "performs" their disability constantly in everyday existence, suggesting that theatre—in some form—is a part of everyday life for a person with a disability.

Other essays in this issue ask us to look at theatre history with fresh eyes and, in some cases, reconsider what we thought to be true. Casey Papas' "The Case for *Machinal*'s Inspiration from *The Subway*" offers a detailed analysis of the similarities between Sophie Treadwell's landmark play and Elmer Rice's forgotten work. Through close reading, parallels emerge between the two works regarding character and structure. However, questions remain. Is "plagiarism" an accurate term to define the relationship between the two plays? Is "inspired by" too simple to define the plot points that are closely connected? What can we learn from these similarities in current theatre practice which borrows constantly from previous works?

Continuing this discussion of theatre history, Shelby Lunderman's "(Re)negotiating Democracy and Theatre" discusses Hallie Flanagan Davis and her aim to invoke antiquity in the strategic planning of The Federal Theatre Project. Flanagan Davis drew inspiration from the Greeks not simply for plays to produce but the role in which theatre played in a democracy. Flanagan Davis' idealism was never fully realized, but there are still lessons to learn about theatre's vital role in a democratic society. Her arguments ring true today as we still aim for theatre that makes an important impact within communities—making audience members into citizens. Similarly, Aubrey Helene Neuman delves into another forgotten era of theatre history: Edward Gordon Craig's two-year break from theatre. During this time, he created a series of woodcut prints, including several of famed actress Ellen Terry—his mother. He re-imagined his mother's celebrated career and image through these art nouveau prints. These years also fostered his future theories on theatre and directorial work, so this time was not wasted but an incubator for another evolution in his career.

For my first volume as a Co-Editor, I am pleased to share this variety of essays, reviews, and interviews to our readers. The contributors to this journal demonstrate the breadth of conversations occurring in theatre practice, representation, and education. As we continue to scrutinize our work as educators and practitioners, let's continue to remember that our work—and our ways of discussing theatre—is an open-ended question.

SHELBY-ALLISON HIBBS
Co-Editor, Texas Theatre Journal

x

On the Cover

Two photographs related to the renowned Federal Theatre
Project make up the front and back covers of this volume
of *Texas Theatre Journal*. On the front, a photograph of
Hallie Flanagan, National Director of the Federal Theatre
Project, speaking on CBS Radio as part of the *Federal
Theatre of the Air* (George Mason University Federal
Theatre project collection).

The back cover features a photo from the FTP's children's theatre production, *The Revolt of the Beavers,* a production which critic Brooks Atikinson called "Marxism à la Mother Goose," and which the House on Un-American Activities Committee used as evidence of the Federal Theatre Project's communist sympathies.

Shelby Lunderman's article on Flanagan, the Federal Theatre Project, and the Dies Commission is just one of many articles in this issue which provide both a deep-dive into and a re-investigation of history.

As an official publication of the Texas Educational Theatre Association, we look to this particularly-history-heavy volume with the eyes of educators and scholars who sincerely believe we can build toward a better future by learning from the past. To quote Mary Anderson and Billicia Hines' wonderful piece on Dominque Morisseau, we hope theatre students, educators, and artists will continue to "participate in a complex choreographed dance between the past and present, between fiction and non-fiction in which the affective space of shame can be unearthed, encountered, and mined as a form of restorative justice." Some may find it a tall order to ask of theatre—but why else would we do what we do?

Texas Theatre Journal
Volume 16 | Fall, 2019

Contents

IT HAPPENS HERE:
ENACTING CHANGE THROUGH
THEATRE EDUCATION

Amanda Rose Villarreal
University of Colorado Boulder

It Happens Here: Project Background

Shortly after the New York Times broke news detailing the allegations against Harvey Weinstein and Bill O'Reilly, the news also broke into my Acting I classroom. My students were presenting scenes when a member of the class, whom I will call J, interrupted two girls in the midst of a scene. "Fucking Shit!" he shouted. I asked if he was alright; interrupting scene work was uncommon in my class. J reacted with an elevated voice laden with expletives, exclaiming that women were lying and accusing helpless men of assault here on campus, when—in his mind—we were all aware that "that shit don't happen here." I engaged J in de-escalation, and invited the class to have a conversation about the topic. He admitted that the recent news and the newly trending (at that time) #MeToo was infuriating for him, and he began to calm down, but he would not listen to the viewpoints of his peers; he insisted that sexual assault only happens in Hollywood. The discussion was tense, but respectful. When class ended, I went directly to the Phoenix Center—the on-campus office for interpersonal violence—to seek advice. It was in that office, speaking with the PCA's assistant director Elizabeth Amoah-Awua, that *It Happens Here* was born. This project, a collaboration between the Community College of Denver's (CCD) theatre department and the Phoenix Center of Auraria (PCA), was a three-tiered performance project designed specifically to engage our students in a safe and open dialogue about sexual assault. *It Happens Here* incorporated performances and postings created by CCD students, and public conversations hosted by students from throughout campus—including a final conversation led by PCA staff and counselors—to engage more members of our campus in dialogue about interpersonal violence within our community; and it worked.

By utilizing performances and interactive events that engage our student body both emotionally and intellectually, theatre educators can create spaces for social activism and debate that are not established through the typical use of lectures, presentations, and workshops which place staff and faculty in the position of moral authority over our students. *It Happens Here* aimed to host educational experiences and active learning, rather than lectures, to increase engagement with topics of violence and assault while endowing students with the ability to facilitate these discussions. On the Auraria campus, these types of conversations are frequently driven by the PCA, which hosts workshops about assault and interpersonal violence on a weekly basis on our campus. However, during the 2016-17 and 2017-18 academic years, these events were attended by an average of eight students[1]. To promote participation in their workshops, the PCA posts informational fliers in bathroom stalls throughout campus advertising these events. However, according to generational learning expert Jason Dorsey, Digital Natives, currently the majority of the Auraria campus's student body, actually prefer—and react better to—face-to-face interaction, both in education and in advertising.[2]

My students and I wanted to both increase the amount of student participation by numbers, as well as to shift the dialogue from PCA staff-led workshops to student-driven discussions. Therefore, we crafted a three-prong project that moved away from the PCA's past practices: *It Happens Here* included performances, in-person conversations, and anonymous interactions crafted to raise awareness of the presence of interpersonal violence upon our campus. Movements like #MeToo facilitate difficult conversations in anonymous outlets which provide individuals with "critical freedom to tell their truth, free from judgement or interruption," which encourages higher rates of social activism within a community.[3] In order to similarly stimulate student involvement, *It Happens Here* included an anonymous written forum that was used to drive a large discussion at the culmination of the project. By utilizing interactive performances, student-led discussions, and anonymous postings for interaction, *It Happens Here* increased on-campus participation in critical conversations. Furthermore, *It Happens Here* engaged students in leading a dialogue throughout the campus, rather than sequestering conversations about this topic to lectures led by staff and faculty.

Enacting Change: Theories in Performance and Education

Educational theorist John Dewey's theory of Transformative Experiential Learning[4] states that learning processes in teens and adults differ drastically from those in children; providing new information is only one aspect of adolescent and adult learning processes. Because adults have already formed their world views, new information which destabilizes their perspective can be subconsciously viewed as threatening and is therefore discarded. According to Dewey, adolescents and adults learn most effectively when learning becomes a social process; discourse with others allows "new information [to] be incorporated by the learner into an already well-developed symbolic frame of reference, an active process involving thought, feelings, and disposition."[5] Dewey writes that we learn best when involved directly in experiencing a problem firsthand, from multiple frames of reference, and working to parse the different aspects of said problem in order to solve it. Transformative Experiential Learning creates lasting effects when the students are not only intellectually, but also emotionally, engaged; "in fact emotions are qualities [...] of a complex experience that moves and changes."[6] *It Happens Here* used performances and discussions to create opportunities for both emotional and intellectual engagement, which according to Dewey, contributes to an "experiential continuum"[7] which increases retention and leads to change—especially in comparison to learning via lecture.[8]

Beginning this project, I wanted to provide my community college students with a foundation of performance-based political activism that precedes them. We discussed Chilean activism group Colectivo de Acciones de Arte (CADA)'s *No Mas* campaign, which focused on guiding citizens to acknowledge the negative aspects of their communities and to challenge, rather than passively support, this negativity. During this campaign, CADA posted the open-ended statement "No Mas"–translating to "no more"–throughout Chilean cities, and the slogan's incomplete nature seemed to invite others to finish the sentence. Completing the phrase required individuals to reflect upon and identify a negative aspect of life within their community. *It Happens Here* used CADA's tactics of publicly posting open-ended phrases to motivate our students to participate in identifying problems, thinking critically about our community, and speaking up throughout the project. The use of postings provided an outlet for students to name their experiences, demonstrate solidarity, and reflect upon negative aspects of their society. This aspect of *It Happens Here* followed in CADA's footsteps, but with an acute awareness of our era and the perception of increased safety within anonymous communications.[9]

My students were particularly inspired by the bold and visceral embodiment of Ana Mendieta's "Untitled (Rape Scene)" which was created "as a reaction against the idea of violence against women."[10] This photograph is the documentation of a tableaux performance which stimulated its audience to discuss assault and violence, as we wished to do. The Tate Gallery describes this project, stating that Mendieta left her dorm room door open, so that her peers—in passing by—could see her in a staged recreation of a recent rape and murder as it had been reported to the media.

According to the exhibition catalogue titled *Ana Mendieta*, the artist herself stated that the witnesses "all sat down, and started talking about it. I didn't move."[11] Mendieta's desire to elicit a visceral reaction from her audience was accomplished through her intensely demanding dedication to physical strain, stillness, and self-exposure. I would never ask my own students to replicate this aspect of her performance; however, we discussed her work, and discussed ways to create visceral responses and facilitate conversation as she did. My students, the performers, determined that representations of violence were necessary, and so we collaborated with a fight choreographer and used Theatrical Intimacy Education's intimacy choreography practices[12] throughout our process to establish a safe devising environment. Together, the students created and rehearsed believable choreography that could potentially trigger strong reactions from our audience, in hopes that witnesses would be willing to sit down and discuss the performances afterwards, as Mendieta's audience had.

It Happens Here Phase 1: The Performances

I facilitated the process, ensuring that my students were engaged in developing *It Happens Here*; together, they created three different types of performances and crafted specific sets of talkback questions to guide conversations in the community. The students scripted and choreographed scenes portraying relationship violence, street harassment, and stalking. Each type of performance was performed, simultaneously at three different locations on campus, to increase our audience size and impact. Following the performances, witnesses were interviewed and invited to the PCA's final conversation. This in-person approach engaged students in leading a dialogue throughout the campus and in the open, rather than sequestering conversations about this topic to lectures led by staff and faculty.

While all of the *It Happens Here* performances led to active participation in discussions, the street harassment performances yielded especially fruitful conversations. The simultaneous street harassment performances began with the character "Victim" minding his or her own business, oblivious to the fact that the character "Photographer" was surreptitiously taking photographs of Victim's physique. Once the photographs were acquired, Photographer began to show the pictures to nearby witnesses—students, faculty, or staff uninvolved with the performance. Once Victim realized what had occurred, he or she left the location to walk across campus to the Tivoli building; en route, Victim was catcalled loudly and from a distance by the character titled "Catcall". Then, "Groper" grasped Victim's arm, stopping them, holding them in place, and loudly commented on Victim's body. Once Victim broke free of Groper's grasp, Victim picked up the pace, being catcalled and laughed at by a trio "Group Catcall" within the campus's main building.

One such performance featured a female student, F, as Victim; in this case, a nearby student approached the Victim and informed her that photos were being taken. F immediately left the coffee shop and walked through campus to the main building; on her route, another student approached Groper to intervene. After F passed their locations, the other performers announced the planned nature of the performance and facilitated discussions. Several students who had witnessed the performance moved back to the coffee shop to share ideas around being active bystanders. One student who had intervened stated that she believes women need to identify the types of unwanted behavior that they see perpetrated towards others; the ongoing process of identification, she said, "will make it less possible for [society and individuals] to ignore or accept [unwanted behavior]." [13] Other students agreed and, throughout the conversation, requested that the PCA host workshops—perhaps during Freshman Orientation—about how to appropriately be an active bystander.

In crafting these performances, my students and I hoped to create an opportunity to discuss the biases that color social reactions to assault, especially regarding the gender spectrum and perceived gender identities. A street harassment performance which occurred simultaneously on the opposite side of campus featured a male student—S—as Victim, and the results varied dramatically. Similarly, a photograph was taken and S walked away, receiving catcalls en route to the main building. When the photos taken were shown to bystanders, students laughed along with Photographer or reacted with surprise, silently moving away or putting hands out to avoid him. No students intervened on behalf of S; instead, the focus was given largely to the student playing Photographer, M. The scene occurred in a pizza shop on campus, and students stared at M or turned and whispered to one another, without intervening. When S was catcalled and touched by other performers, students in the vicinity silently exchanged glances, laughed uncomfortably, or whispered to one another.

When the actors interviewed individual witnesses and brought students into a conversation, the witnesses' reaction was one of confusion. Many students stated that they weren't sure what was happening. One student, who was shown a close-up photograph of S butt, said that she thought the two were friends and one was just trying to embarrass the other. She admitted that it never occurred to her that a male identifying individual whose photograph was taken would be impacted the same way that a female identifying person would be, if put in the same situation.[14] This was echoed by others in the group who had witnessed the performance; the concept that a male could be the target of street harassment was so boggling that the students struggled to understand the scenes unfolding in front of them. One student who witnessed S and M's performance said that seeing the events felt "surreal, like, I mean, I've been there and I know how it feels to have that happen, but I just didn't connect. Because, I mean, who does that?"[15] The students—twelve in total—

discussed the concept that maybe men who engage in street harassment have the same bewildered or disconnected reaction when talking to victims, having never been targeted themselves. Meanwhile, S was heavily impacted by the experience, and shared his reactions with the group, saying "I felt so helpless, out of my body, you know? Even though we rehearsed and I knew what was coming, when I looked around and everybody seemed like they were in on it I just felt like I was shrinking." Hearing his reaction, many female students in the discussion group nodded; some of the male students questioned him, seeking details about what it felt like. One student said that it was "more comfortable to ask a dude" and to learn about his experience, than to ask a female peer.

Including the unmentioned performances and the following discussions, our performers and PCA student workers facilitated conversations with 72 students over the course of two weeks. Students were leading the conversations themselves, actively connecting with one another and with the content being discussed. Witnessing these performances in-person and engaging in face-to-face analysis of the performances and society allowed the students to learn—as humans do best— through experience.[16] Witnessing an emotionally heated event and delving into deep criticism of their culture, the students were engaged in Dewey's Transformative Experiential Learning process, initiated by the performances and led by the students themselves

It Happens Here: The Postings

The second part of this project—inspired by CADA's *No Mas* postings—sought to include the entire campus in the *It Happens Here* project. In creating the postings, theatre students and the PCA staff endeavored to create a format through which students could engage in a conversation in a comfortable manner—especially for those who fear openly divulging information. Therefore, we created large, plywood posters that were located in high-traffic areas on campus, each with attached markers and invitations for anyone passing by to write upon the postings. This allowed us to create an offline space for students to engage with one another and the community that immediately surrounds them, with all of the anonymity that makes online interaction appealing for so many.

When we conceptualized the idea of the posters, we also hoped to create a visual representation of the prevalence of violence within our campus and community, in order to combat the adoption of the "Just World Fallacy", a logical fallacy which "imperils the relational equality required for shared participation in communities."[17] The Just World Fallacy occurs when citizens adopt the belief that their surroundings are safe and organized towards justice, allowing them to dismiss instances of violence that they see as entirely out of the ordinary.[18] This leads to the mindset that

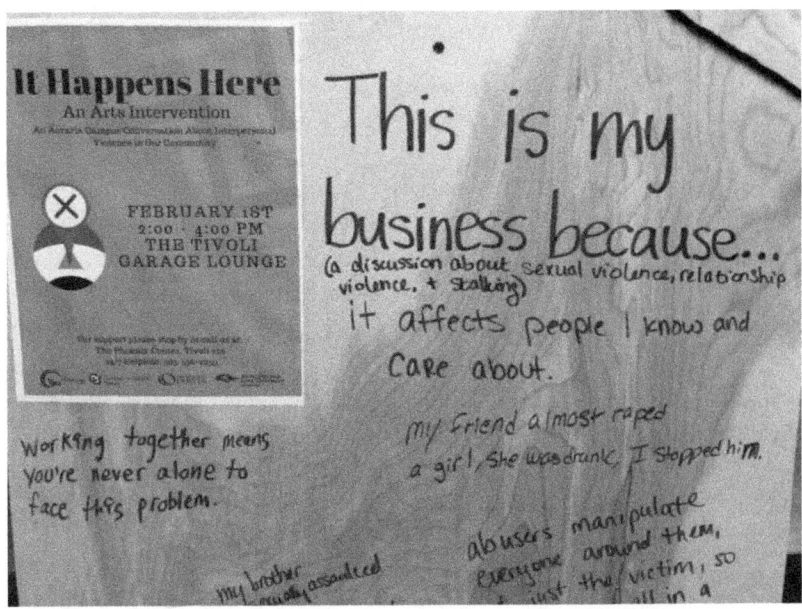

Fig. 1. Image from the *It Happens Here* postings at the University of Colorado Boulder, featuring comments written by students and passersby. Image provided by author, used by permission.

unnecessary violence does not occur in our immediate surroundings, but only in communities that are both morally corrupt and far removed from our own experience. By establishing large-scale physical reminders of the prevalence of violence within our own community, we hoped to confront our campus with unavoidable evidence that it does, in fact, happen here. With this in mind, we created posters which featured the prompts "Assault Is..." "I Wish People Knew..." "It's My Business Because..." and "Take Up Space; Leave Your Mark." These posters became the grounds for revelatory conversations which instigated further discussion during the third phase—public conversations—of *It Happens Here.*

The "Assault Is" postings around campus—three in total—created an interesting dialogue that included interpersonal debates. One posting, located outside of the library, was eight feet long and three feet tall; the entire piece of lumber was filled with commentary from the community. Someone had completed the prompt with the statement "Terrorism." A new set of handwriting added "against women," and a third individual responded with "yup, just women *glares*" and yet a fourth comment, still in new handwriting, summarized by stating "unacceptable, no matter what gender you are." This exchange, which happened anonymously, demonstrates that four individuals, with different biases and viewpoints, engaged in critical conversations about assault.

Similarly differing viewpoints were expressed on other "Assault Is" postings around campus. One, located in the Tivoli building, featured the word "awesome" written in bright purple ink; the community's response was to scribble the word out with red marker, and write "disgusting" above the comment in dark blue ink. A similar exchange occurred on a posting in the King Center, where someone wrote in black marker "Fuck you bitches," to which the community responded by writing comments and using arrows to direct these statements to the aforementioned aggression. One person wrote "doesn't get it," while another responded, "no just a asshole." Yet another person responded with "Why so defensive? Do you feel guilty? It's ok, we're not gonna attack you back, so let's talk about it, okay?" Each of these examples indicates community members with different perspectives actively engaging in dialogue to educate their peers and support others within their community.

The anonymous nature of the *It Happens Here* postings not only allowed for critical debate to emerge; they offered an opportunity for victims to vent and self-identify, which is an important step in the healing process.[19] Comments such as:

"(Assault is) 20 years and still feeling like I can't share what's happened,"

"(I wish people knew) the sound of a woman's voice echoes in my head because of not intervening" as well as

"(Assault is) the reason I had to drop out," and

"(This is my business because) We dated for 3 years but she still emotionally and physically abused me"

illustrate different personal experiences that impact the Auraria community, some of which could invert common gendered assumptions and biases about assault. We do not know the authors of these comments, nor the stories behind them, but PCA assistant director Elizabeth Amoah-Awua said that such self-disclosure rarely occurs in PCA workshops outside of group therapy. The anonymous performance of writing on the postings, then, likely encouraged these individuals to engage in the conversation surrounding assault and violence in our community.

It Happens Here: Educational Outcomes

With the PCA staff advising in the creation of the postings and overseeing the final public conversation—the third phase of this project—we ensured that *It Happens Here* aligned with their office's mission. The Phoenix Center focuses on interpersonal violence (IPV) prevention, and its mission statement emphasizes an active approach to this goal, stating that the office seeks to "implement campus response services, provide education, and facilitate dialogue related to IPV in the Auraria community"[20] The PCA's typical approach to serving the Auraria community and following this mission uses restroom postings—infographics regarding interpersonal violence statistics, resources, and stories which are posted inside restroom stall doors—to reach a wide audience on campus. This meets the goal of providing education; however, according to both John Dewey's research and *Adult Learners: A Neglected Species*, the presence of information alone does not lead to education.[21] Both Dewey and Knowles write that, in order to learn and grow, the learner must engage with experiences that reinforce the information provided or connect said information to their lives.[22, 23] *It Happens Here* did just that; by allowing witnesses to engage with the performances and reflect upon the events afterwards, we facilitated learning that aligned with a continuum of experiences for our community. The performative aspects of this project—both the devised performances and the embodiment of thought through the process of writing upon a posting—engaged learners in transformative experiences that illustrate the benefits of using theatre to enhance learning in other subject areas.

   It Happens Here provided an important inter-departmental learning opportunity, as well. According to educational researcher Eric Toshalis, silos form when professionals and learners primarily interact with others who share an ideological belief system; for example, when teachers rely only on other teachers as resources, or when theatre practitioners only interact with other artists. Toshalis writes that learning in ideologically isolated environments is harmful, because "despite the fact that progress depends on a research-proven, field-tested, policy-driven evidence base, the lack of coordination and collaboration across these sectors [keeps] us from moving the field forward."[24] However, *It Happens Here* allowed the PCA and the theatre department to collaboratively create socially impactful experiences for their community. K, a graduating theatre major who devised and performed in this project, wrote in her final reflection that she "didn't really know that people were doing projects like this. I'm so excited that I can learn to mix my passions theatre and social justice together!"[25] This project fit into my students' continuum of experiences,[26] connecting the work they had done in the past to new possibilities for work in their future. By creating and performing new pieces based on their concerns for their community, my students broadened their awareness of career possibilities within arts and public activism while developing self-starting, advocating artistic tendencies. M's first reflection reflects this growth, stating: "I feel like this kind of art empowers me to take a stand in my community, for people who are Arabic and Muslim like me, and for people who are attacked for other reasons. It's hard for me to speak up as [myself], but doing it as a character with an ensemble makes me feel empowered to do what I usually wouldn't."[27] Meanwhile, another student's final reflection said "I wish all learning included projects with the community like this because now I feel so much more prepared to not just find a job but to make things happen in my life."[28]

By breaking the mold of working in silos within higher education and partnering the CCD theatre department with the PCA, we created an innovative approach to facilitating discussion around sexual assault. By utilizing performance within this project, we were able to engage students throughout campus emotionally and intellectually and encourage those students to discuss interpersonal violence with peers from other academic silos, which deepened the conversation. By using public postings to allow for anonymous interaction, we decreased the affective filter of students on campus, creating engagement opportunities for those who are introverted or otherwise intimidated by the topic of sexual assault. By using theatre to create educational experiences, we supported the mission and educational goals of the PCA, illustrating that theatre enhances learning in other content areas. *It Happens Here* created new opportunities for students to learn and to lead in ways that siloed conversations, lectures, and workshops would not.

---

[1] Elizabeth Amoah-Awua, Follow-up Meeting at the Phoenix Center at Auraria, In Person, Voice Recording, February 16, 2018.

[2] TEDx Talks, *What Do We Know about the Generation after Millennials? | Jason Dorsey | TEDxHouston*, accessed March 14, 2018, https://www.youtube.com/watch?v=4f16o9Q0XGE.

[3] Emma Hyndman, "The Invisible #MeToo: How Anonymous Testimony Can Help Survivors of Sexual Abuse," Open Democracy, November 16, 2017, https://www.opendemocracy.net/5050/emma-hyndman/invisible-metoo-anonymous-testimony-sexual-abuse.

[4] John Dewey, *Experience & Education* (New York, NY: Free Press, 1938) 25-50.

[5] Jack Mezirow, "Transformative Learning: Theory to Practice," *New Directions for Adult and Continuing Education* 1997, no. 74 (1997): 5–12, https://doi.org/10.1002/ace.7401.

[6] John Dewey, *Art as Experience* (London, England: Penguin Books Ltd, 1934) 43.

[7] Ibid., 28.

[8] Ibid., 89.

[9] Emma Hyndman, "The Invisible #MeToo: How Anonymous Testimony Can Help Survivors of Sexual Abuse."

[10] Olga Viso, *Unseen Mendieta: The Unpublished Works of Ana Mendieta* (Munich: Prestel USA, 2008) 256.

[11] Fundacio Antoni Tapies, *Ana Mendieta, Exhibition Catalogue* (Barcelona: Centro Galego de Arte Contemporánea, 1996).

[12] Chelsea Pace, "Theatrical Intimacy Education," Theatrical Intimacy Education, 2018, https://www.theatricalintimacyed.com/.

[13] Various, Student Interviews: Street Harrassment, January 29, 2018 (Recording 1) 19:13.

[14] Various, Student Interviews: Street Harrassment, January 29, 2018 (Recording 3) 7:22.

[15] Ibid., 4:19.

[16] Dewey, *Experience & Education* 25.

[17] Matthew Sinnicks, "The Just World Fallacy as a Challenge to the Business-As-Community Thesis:," *Business & Society*, February 26, 2018, https://doi.org/10.1177/0007650318759486.

[18] Sinnicks.

[19] Hyndman, "The Invisible #MeToo: How Anonymous Testimony Can Help Survivors of Sexual Abuse."

[20] "The Phoenix Center at Auraria," *The Phoenix Center at Auraria – Ending Interpersonal Violence through Prevention, Awareness, and Support Services* (blog), 2017, http://www.thepca.org/.

[21] Malcolm S. Knowles, *The Adult Learner: A Neglected Species*, 2d ed, Building Blocks of Human Potential Series (Houston: Gulf Pub. Co., Book Division, 1978) 95.

[22] Dewey, *Experience & Education* 26.

[23] Knowles, *The Adult Learner* 94-98.

[24] Eric Toshalis, "Breaking Down Silos with the Student-Centered Learning Research Collaborative | Jobs for the Future," http://www.jff.org/blog/2017/01/24/breaking-down-silos-student-centered-learning-research-collaborative.

[25] K Student, "Reflection 3" (D2L, March 17, 2018) 4.

[26] Dewey, *Experience & Education* 25.

[27] M Student, "Reflection 1" (D2L, February 18, 2018).

[28] S Student, "Reflection 3" (D2L, March 17, 2018).

CRIPPED VISUALITY:
SHIFTING VISUAL CULTURE
OF DISABILITY IN ONE-WOMAN
SHOWS

Nicholas Shannon Savard
The Ohio State University

From a dark stage, we hear a woman sing a slow melody about a friend who has asked her for advice after being diagnosed with an illness; she's searching for it still. The music picks up; slowly the lights come up and Anita Hollander walks to center stage, singing about how she's been told she has courage, not believing it, and receiving the insight that "courage is actually made from your darkest fear." She continues, "so here I stand, and not much less afraid than I was before. Here I stand, but now I know just a little more." The music picks up, Hollander lifts her skirt, loudly rips the Velcro wrapped around her waist, props herself up on a stool center stage, and removes her hip-height, nylon and high heel-clad prosthetic leg. On beat, she stomps it on the floor, smiling up at the audience.

This is one of two images that reviewers of Hollander's one-woman show, *Still Standing*, consistently claim characterize the piece.[1] The other image critics seem drawn to is one of Hollander with her artificial limb hanging "at a jaunty angle" over her shoulder.[2] *Still Standing* is a musical autobiographical account of Hollander's experience as a self-described one-legged actor from the moment she was diagnosed with a cancerous tumor in her left leg up to the current moment as she stands before the audience.[3] While all of the reviews of her 2019 run at Boston's New Repertory Theatre acknowledge Hollander's role as a disability activist, none address the specific impact of the way in which she chooses to make her amputee status visible. Rather than simply exposing her left leg as a prosthetic, she removes the limb entirely, revealing her disabled body. However, her smile and her stomping of a leg that is no longer attached to her body set a playful tone for the rest of the opening number. Hollander's storytelling combined with the physical relationship she sets up between her body and her prosthetic leg works to both reveal existing cultural narratives about amputees and disrupts any opportunity for the audience to read those narratives onto her. She undermines the narrative of struggle, illness, and fear that she established in the first verse. In that moment, Hollander denies her audience the option of reading a typical "tragic" narrative of disability onto her body, instead inviting them to re-imagine their own definition of what life with a disability is to include play and laughter.

Performers like Hollander—and as I will describe later, Kristina Wong—use disability aesthetics and cripped performance practices to intervene into dominant cultural visual narratives which shape the collective imagination of what disability is and what it looks like in order to offer their audiences alternative visual narratives which complicate or completely subvert preconceived notions. When disability aesthetics and cripped performance practices converge in the intimate setting of live solo performance, disabled theatre artists and their audiences enter into a space where normative understandings of bodies, impairment, and disability become unstable. In that moment of confrontation, cultural interrogation, and challenge to visual expectations, the performer and the audience can co-construct new disability visualities. This encounter between the audience and the disabled performer[4] produces what I call cripped visuality.

References to "crip," "cripping," and "cripped," here, come out of the reclamation of the pejorative "cripple" which has historically cast people with disabilities as inherently deficient, tragic, and isolated from their communities. Crip theory—as opposed to person-first language which emphasizes the person over their disability—embraces disability as an integral part of both individual and shared experience and identity, drawing upon and building from Disability Studies, queer theory, feminist theory, and Critical Race Theory. Disability Studies scholar Georgina Kleege defines visuality as "the cultural practices and values related to vision and the making of mental images of abstract ideas." Within the context of Disability Studies, visuality encompasses both visibility and invisibility or, more specifically, "qualities in an individual's embodiment or physical behavior through which impairment is made visually manifest." Based on this emphasis on the visual perceptibility of impairment, Kleege notes that people with "invisible" impairments tend to be excluded when the general public imagines disability.[5] While Anita Hollander challenges the dominant imagery surrounding physically disabled people, Kristina Wong's *Wong Flew Over the Cuckoo's Nest* sheds light on and complicates cultural perceptions of mental illness. Since visuality is produced through collective imagination, it is inherently embedded in culture. As Disability Studies scholars Lennard Davis and Marquard Smith explain, "visuality is both determined by and determining of our understanding of disability."[6] This mutually constitutive relationship between collective imagination, disabled bodies, embodied experience, and social visibility mean that disability visuality is constantly being constructed. Theatrical performance has the potential to offer an opportunity to reveal the instability of normative visualities and produce new, "cripped" visualities in audiences. Visuality for theatre audiences in this case might most productively be understood as the narratives the dominant culture will allow spectators to read onto a performer's body. Visuality is typically a conservative force which constructs social narratives and attempts to maintain stable visual and conceptual categories (i.e. man, woman, black, white, disabled, ablebodied). When the cultural narratives about disability and disabled people are disrupted, twisted, or complicated, the spectators must either attempt to fit those alternatives into their existing understandings or revise their understanding to include a different experience. Cripped visuality is produced in that moment of revision.

Cripped visuality is the effect produced by a performative act in which a disabled person displays their embodied experience in a way that subverts, challenges, spins, or elucidates the dominant cultural narratives and images of disability. The act is intentionally public and confronts the spectator in such a way that they must directly engage with the performer's disabled bodymind[7] and their own assumptions, stereotypes, and mental imagery. The performance itself is an emphatic disruption of normative disability visuality, and as a result of the performer's "cripping," audience member's understandings of disability and the imagery and narratives available to them become "cripped."

Cripped performance is closely aligned with disability aesthetics. Tobin Siebers writes that disability aesthetics works on multiple levels, "affirming that disability may operate both as a critical framework for questioning aesthetic presuppositions in the history of art and as a value in its own right, important to future conceptions of what art is."[8] In theatrical settings, disabled performance artists themselves exhibit their bodies as aesthetic objects and at the same time, according to Johnson Cheu in his article "Performing Disability, Problematizing Cure," they allow their bodies to serve as a metaphor or as a representational system of experiences which "revolves not around impairment, but around cultural responses to impairment."[9] "Cripping" as a performative act seeks to highlight those cultural responses to the disabled body.

In the opening number of *Still Standing*, Hollander illustrates how the general public responds to her disability by comparing her experience of navigating the world as an amputee with and without her prosthetic. She sings, "I live in New York City and get mugged on two legs, but I don't get mugged on one. And the guys who mug me see me on one leg and say 'God bless you, hon.' I don't stand in line at the bank or post office if someone sees me there." These lines reveal what lies in the collective imagination about amputees through Hollander's interactions in public spaces: amputees are assumed to be weak and worthy of pity. She does not dispute this, instead choosing to complicate the image of her on one leg and crutches by adding the threat: "And I've got two strong metal weapons for anyone who thinks that's unfair." In this moment she both brings forth the dominant image of a physically disabled person and twists it to make her crutches—one of the visual markers of her disability—a source of power. Hollander's contrast of the dominant narrative surrounding disabled people and her own reinterpretation illustrate what Carrie Sandahl calls "cripping" in performance. In "Queering the Crip or Cripping the Queer? Intersections of Queer and Crip Identities in Solo Autobiographical Performance," Sandahl draws parallels between the performance of cripping and queering in that each "spins mainstream representations or practices to reveal able-bodied assumptions or exclusionary effects." She continues, "Both queering and cripping expose the arbitrary delineation between normal and defective and negative social ramifications of attempts to homogenize humanity, and both disarm what is painful with wicked humor including camp."[10] Sandahl's description of cripping depends on the performer's radical resistance of normalcy through their insistence on making themselves visible as disabled persons and artists.

Hollander continues reframing the ableist understanding of her life as an amputee by listing the benefits she finds in having one leg, including having more room in airplane seats, only needing to shave one leg and buy one sock, and having a perfect spot to keep her popcorn warm at the movie theatre (on the seat, nestled by her left hip socket). As the music slows, Hollander again acknowledges that the experience that she has presented does not align with the typical image of how an amputee is expected to relate to their prosthetic limb. "Now I know some amputees don't quite agree with me—They wear theirs each day," she sings, grabbing her prosthetic and holding it in the air, revealing that for her it is, in fact, an active choice for her not to pass as able-bodied. In the final line of the song she belts out, "And there's one thing left to say. I'm more comfortable this way," as she gleefully lifts up her prosthetic leg and slings it over her shoulder. Hollander's glee in describing her experience and her playfulness in interacting with her prosthetic brings the flow of dominant visual narratives surrounding amputees and the pity and tragedy they invoke to a complete halt. She refuses the audience the option of reading those normative narratives onto her. The joy that she exudes is not in spite of her disability; this would fall into the common narrative of "overcoming" limitations. Rather, she displays happiness in her performance through her interaction with a removed prosthetic limb and highlights the utter contrast between how she experiences her own body and the way that the general public reacts to her body. At once she makes the audience aware of existing cultural narratives, which are often naturalized and unquestioned, and makes it impossible for them to fit her body into the collective imagination's picture of what it is to be an amputee.

Throughout the remainder of the show, Hollander troubles the relationship between her body and her prosthetic limb. At various moments she makes the leg dance, stands or sits it on the stool, leaves it abandoned across the stage, and physically deconstructs it to its various parts. Rather than a tool or replacement for a natural limb, Hollander treats her prosthetic as a prop. It is often entirely separate from her body as opposed to a synthetic extension to make her appear able-bodied or to approximate the normative model of bodily wholeness. In her use of her prosthetic for alternative purposes she emphasizes its inanimate nature and forces her audience to view it as an object. The more odd positions she places it in, the more disconnected from her person the prosthetic leg becomes. She draws attention to the fact that her prosthetic, which passes for a "real" leg in the streets of New York, is a piece of technology. In defiant opposition to the expectation that she use her prosthetic to give her body a more socially acceptable impression of "wholeness," Hollander uses it as a plaything that she can manipulate to amuse herself, choosing to present herself in a way that attends to her own comfort and pleasure rather than managing the discomfort and stares of others.

Because Hollander engages in storytelling informed by her own embodied experience and directly addresses the audience throughout the show, she establishes an intimate relationship with them where they are invited to stare at her and her body in ways that would be socially inappropriate in other contexts. This convention makes autobiographical solo performance a particularly generative site for producing cripped visuality. As Rosemarie Garland-Thomson explains in *Staring, How We Look,* a disabled person can stage "strategic staring encounters" in which the stare leads their audience to convert their immediate curiosity or disgust in viewing something unexpected to attention and engagement. Garland-Thomson specifically describes how author and disability rights activist Harriet McBryde Johnson manages these staring encounters: "She moves the audience from what they do not expect to see to perhaps expecting to see people like her again. In other words, she gets them accustomed to looking at her by making herself more familiar than strange, by bringing her life story closer to their own."[11] The relationship that the one-person show establishes with the audience invites extended visual engagement with the performer's disabled bodymind without the voyeuristic nature of realism-inspired theatre or film. Autobiographical performance closes the aesthetic distance that fiction offers the audience in favor of acknowledging the artists' own lived experiences and bringing attention to the bodies in the room as well as the cultural narratives they carry.

Cripped visuality is not necessarily dependent entirely on the visual or the visible. Rather, an artist might use cripped performance in order to make an "invisible" disability legible to the audience. According to Tobin Siebers' "Disability as Masquerade," people with disabilities are always performing their disability whether attempting to conceal it by "passing" as able-bodied or "masquerading" their disability.[12] The body itself, rather than the signs of disability, becomes the conveyor of a visual narrative. The disability masquerade is a process through which a disabled person intentionally performs markers of their disability in order to assure it can be read and understood by others, regardless of whether their bodymind fits the dominant cultural image of how someone their particular disability ought to look and act. In *Wong Flew Over the Cuckoo's Nest*, Kristina Wong produces cripped visualities in performing her own version of disability masquerade to make her doubly culturally invisible identities, as an Asian American woman with depression, legible to her audience. Wong's performance demands that her depression is read by the audience, asks that they incorporate her body into their concept of how depression looks, and reveals the process of disability masquerade she has had to perform in order to access mental health-related care in the United States. Throughout the performance, she calls attention to the high rates of depression and suicide among Asian American women, interrogates common cultural narratives and stereotypes about Asian American women and depression, and elucidates multiple ways in which her racial identity and mental illness intersect, conflict, and complicate one another through storytelling.[13]

In the opening moments of her 2013 performance, directed by Michael Closson and recorded for DVD, Wong introduces her topic: the high rates of depression and suicide among Asian American women. She assures the audience that she is uniquely qualified to solve this crisis because, of course, she has never experienced depression herself. She adds that, in fact, none of the women in the Wong family have ever been depressed, and, actually, neither has anyone of Chinese descent. Her quick dive into hyperbole hints at the reality of the familial and culturally-enforced silence surrounding mental illness within the Asian American community. The contradiction between the problem that she lays out and her over-emphasis that people like her do not suffer from depression set Wong up as an unreliable narrator. In a review of the show, Michelle Carlson of Hyphen Magazine wrote, "As the audience watches her unravel over the course of the show, she shifts back and forth between being the subject and the object of her own performance. Instead of finding a tidy conclusion, audience members ask, 'Is this unreliable narrator OK? Is she going to get us out of this crisis?'"[14] To further distance herself from the depressed Asian American women she claims to be saving, Wong insists that all of the stories she tells are fictional. After several scenes where Wong does speak in first person, and appears to be spiraling into a panic, she asks the audience to respond to her question: "Remember, this is what?" by shouting back "fiction." In an interview with the blog *AsAm News*, Wong explained that particular choice:

> I created this preface that the show was 'fiction' as a form of self-preservation. As I developed the show, I realized this idea of 'fiction' was a great metaphor for how depression and suicide manifests in Asian American communities. Asian Americans I know, including myself, tend to 'fictionalize' that anything is going wrong to save face [...] I'd love for audiences to realize that the conceit of the show being about Asian American women is actually more a premise than an outcome. I hope, if anything, they get that it's the fictionalization around depression and the silence around these issues that causes depression and suicide to spike.[15]

By asking the audience members to participate in classifying the story told on stage as fiction, she interpellates them as part of the culture of silence which pressures her to pretend "everything is fine." The unreliability of Wong's persona, however, invites the audience to read against the popular narratives that she presents to them and read her character as speaking from her own experience with depression and working through her own crisis as the story progresses.

When Wong initially visually situates her performance within the traditional dramatic arc (exposition, crisis, rising action, climax, falling action, resolution) by projecting a labeled drawing on a screen, she claims that the crisis for this character will be that she must save all of the depressed Asian American women from killing themselves, represent each and every one of their stories, and do so in a way that will not make the white people in the audience uncomfortable. The stipulations of her goal imply that the problem she describes is not contained within the Asian American community but is heavily influenced by hegemonic white cultural norms and social structures. She forces the members of the audience to take stock of their own subjectivity as they watch her. White audience members, in particular, are asked to confront in that moment both the way that racism impacts Wong's ability to truthfully tell her own story in its entirety and the way that their own attitudes, reactions, and stereotypes may contribute to the way her narrative is constrained and how people of color are frequently silenced across American culture.

In her first explicit moment of cripped performance, Wong challenges the dominant visuality surrounding depression. Each woman that she portrays in the segment following her opening scene is introduced as a series of psychiatric intake notes projected onto a screen behind her. The notes list sex, age, ethnicity, city, and symptoms. The projections imply that the sterile, black and white, reductive psychiatric notes compose existing depression visualities. Wong makes her intervention by giving each woman a name and performing a monologue from her perspective. Depression becomes an embodied reality rather than a list of symptoms. In Wong's monologues, depression is a Cambodian American woman who has not slept in weeks because her baby cries through the night, and she doesn't know what is wrong. It is that same woman's mother who cannot care for her sick infant granddaughter because the doctors do not understand her broken English. It is a refugee who had to flee a war zone without her son or husband and a first- generation American college student who fears that she is wasting her parents' hard-earned money. As the slides begin changing faster and faster, Wong cannot keep up; there are too many women, too much trauma. A fuse blows and the stage goes dark. Wong is left to navigate the stage using only a flashlight.

By taking away the audience's ability to see what is happening on stage, Wong illuminates the barriers she faces in making her own depression visible and getting support from those around her. Neither the audience nor the imagined people she interacts with are able to clearly "see" her; they cannot perceive the details of her crisis, and Wong is left isolated, both visually and emotionally, in coping with it. She shines her flashlight on different articles of clothing hanging from the rafters which stand in for various people in her life and barriers to getting help. An old college friend with a steady job, a baby, a husband, and her own house embodies multiple heteronormative middle class markers of success that Wong does not fit; that friend doesn't have the time to help her through her crisis. Her grandmother, a Chinese American immigrant, is warm and welcoming, and Wong struggles to remember the words to explain her situation; the audience listens to her stumble through slow and uncertain Mandarin phrases which fail to make her grandmother understand. She stops her explanation of the crisis to her mother so as not to worry her. The one-sided conversations she presents reveal several barriers to mental health support between reproductive and capitalist pressures, linguistic barriers, and managing family relationships. Wong's crisis becomes not a merely a personal emotional issue but the result of a series of cultural systems that cannot acknowledge her or offer significant care or support.

In her attempt to find help moving past the crisis stage and completing the dramatic arc, Wong conducts a frantic google search to see how other Asian American women have completed their stories. She first looks to famous actresses like Lucy Liu, whose online biography contains exposition and resolution but no crisis. When she googles Asian American women more generally to find how they got through their crises, she discovers that many of the narratives involved extraordinary traumatic experiences which seem to have brought those women to the adult film industry. At this point, Wong abandons the model of the traditional dramatic arc, and labels the dichotomous nature of visualities surrounding Asian American women drawing two boxes on the overhead projector: "perfect" and "porn." The "perfect" women have never had a crisis, and the women who have survived tragedy apparently end up in "porn." The scene exposes a problem within white hegemonic culture where Asian American women are only granted visibility if they fit into one of those two narrow categories. The perfect/porn binary that Wong sets up in this scene mirrors the dominant stereotypes of Asian women within American culture: the "model minority" and the submissive, hypersexualized woman who is the object of white men's "yellow fever." As a result of the gaps in the collective imagination, the available narratives for Asian American women within the dominant culture are incomplete and flattened, leaving little room to envision complex lives or generate understanding of the high rates of depression among this group of women.

Wong attempts to write her own, unguided, narrative for an Asian American woman who successfully works through her crisis. The next steps, she claims, should not be too difficult. She just has to find a therapist, show up at their office, present her insurance card, and be cured. To further complicate her situation, she makes visible another point of intersectionality impacting her experience and erecting barriers: the fact that she does not have health insurance. In her attempt to access free, state-sponsored mental healthcare, Wong reveals the process of the disability masquerade which she employs to prove her condition is worthy of care and to make her depression legible to a government employee on the other end of the phone line.

In her first phone call to someone that she believes can connect her to state-sponsored free mental healthcare, Wong gives a vulnerable pitch describing her emotional state and attempting to find reasons which justify her depression from family pressures to an instance of sexual assault when she was younger. Over the course of four phone calls, she continues to perform more and more exaggerated versions of the disability masquerade as she is forced to jump through more and more bureaucratic hoops to get in touch with an actual therapist through the government program. Throughout the next three monologues, she describes her situation in increasingly blunt terms and her recounting of her various traumatic incidents becomes more intense; the details get more gruesome and she reports the events happening earlier and earlier in her childhood. She frames the final phone call as the biggest audition of her career: the role of eligible recipient of free state-sponsored healthcare. She asks the audience to help her prepare for the role, making them judge whether or not she seems "crazy enough" to be deserving of the resources she needs. She runs down the center aisle groaning, grunting, and flailing her arms. She stops in front of a white woman in her sixties sitting in the front row, looks her in the eye, and asks, "Would you cast me? Would you cast me now?" The entire front row is sitting straight up in their seats. Their smiles have faded, apart from the occasional uncomfortable laugh. "Clearly you're not convinced." Wong smears lipstick haphazardly around her mouth and groans again, leaning in closer. "Would you cast me now?" The woman nods once, her shoulders and jaw visibly tensed, and Wong returns to the stage to make her final call.

This moment reflects two different purposes of Siebers' disability masquerade. Wong uses the exaggerated performance of her mental illness to put expectations of what her disability ought to look like into her own service.[16] If she can sound like she has experienced enough trauma and has more than enough logical justification to be depressed (according to the presumably non-depressed government official on the phone), she will be more likely to receive the services she needs. The disability masquerade, here, is a strategy to make Wong undeniably legible as a mentally ill person, despite the fact that her daily reality may not align with the general public's conception of what depression ought to look like. In addition, her disability masquerade may "contravene an existing system of oppression."[17] After multiple phone calls over the course of months, the identical scripted responses of the workers at the various call centers, and the repeated performance of trauma and illness, the intense labor of accessing care while poor and uninsured becomes visible to the audience. The purpose of playing up her trauma and depression is not to trick the person on the phone but to provide a better chance of combating class oppression and actually accessing care in a culture that demonizes the poor and only provides the already scarce resources to those deemed most "deserving."

Kristina Wong's performance is at once highly personal and specific and representative of larger issues of racism, cultural expectations, and access. Her cripped visuality for Asian American women with depression demands that the audience consider mental illness in the context of race, ethnicity, class, and language. *Wong Flew Over the Cuckoo's Nest* makes a strong argument that cripped visualities must be intersectional and that the existing cultural narratives of Asian American women and mental illness are woefully incomplete.

The one-person show provides a unique and productive environment for the generation of cripped visualities. Anita Hollander and Kristina Wong play with their audiences' expectations of how a disabled or mentally ill person ought to behave and force them to evaluate and possibly revise previously held beliefs about what life with disabilities looks like. Each of these women confronts her audience in such a way that invites them to stare and to engage with their bodyminds and makes them aware of their own subjectivity and role in co-constructing the narratives of disabled women. In producing cripped visualities with the people in the room, these performances provide a more complicated visual and cultural narrative than those readily available within the public imagination.

[1] Ally Lardner, "One-Woman Show, 'Still Standing,' Intimately Portrays Life of Playwright," *Boston College Heights*, Feb. 21, 2019.

[2] Don Aucoin, "A Personal Story of Disability and Ability in New Rep's 'Still Standing,'" *The Boston Globe*, Feb. 27, 2019.

[3] Anita Hollander, "Still Standing Part 1" and "Still Standing Part 2," *Vimeo*, uploaded by Traffic City Lullaby, 2012, Video, https://vimeo.com/55731792.

[4] I use "disabled performer" here rather than "performer with a disability" to highlight the specific attention the artists I reference throughout this article draw to their disabilities. In each of the performances I examine disability, embodied experience, and social expectations surrounding bodies are the primary focuses of the material. The choice to foreground disabled identities and experiences are intentional political moves which aim to increase visibility.

[5] Georgina Kleege, "Visuality," in Keywords for Disability Studies, ed. Rachel Adams, Benjamin Reiss, and David Serlin (New York: New York University Press, 2015), 182, 184.

[6] Lennard Davis and Marquad Smith, "Editorial: Disability-Visuality," *Journal of Visual Culture* 5, no. 2 (2006): 132.

[7] The term bodymind, introduced by Disability Studies scholar Margaret Price, is used to counteract the implicit division between the body and the mind and to mark the ways in which mental and physical processes both affect and give rise to one another.

[8] Tobin Siebers, "Disability Aesthetics" *PMLA* 120, no. 2 (2005): 546.

[9] Johnson Cheu, "Performing Disability, Problematizing Cure" In *Bodies in Commotion: Disability and Performance*, ed. Philip Auslander and Carrie Sandahl, (Ann Arbor: University of Michigan Press, 2005), 137.

[10] Carrie Sandahl, "Queering the Crip or Cripping the Queer? Intersections of Queer and Crip Identities in Solo Autobiographical Performance," *GLQ: A Journal of Gay and Lesbian Studies* 9, no. 1 (2003): 37.

[11] Rosemarie Garland-Thomson, *Staring, How We Look* (Oxford: Oxford University Press, 2009), 191.

[12] Tobin Siebers, "Disability as Masquerade," *Literature and Medicine* 23, no. 1 (2004): 3-4.

[13] Kristina Wong, *Wong Flew Over the Cuckoo's Nest*, directed by Michael Closson, Cinema Libre Studio, 2013, DVD.

[14] Michelle Carlson, "Wong Knows Best: Kristina Wong confronts power, stereotypes, and racism," *Hyphen Magazine: Asian America Unabridged*, March 30, 2016. https://hyphenmagazine.com/magazine/issue-29-health-issue-fall-2015/wong-knows-best

[15] "Why Wong Flew Over the Cuckoo's Nest," *AsAm News*, Dec. 5, 2013. https://asamnews.com/tag/wong-flew-over-the-cuckoos-nest/

[16] Siebers, "Disability Masquerade," 11.

[17] Ibid., 10.

BURIED UNDERGROUND:

THE CASE FOR *MACHINAL*'S

INSPIRATION FROM *THE SUBWAY*

Casey Papas

Baylor University

Despite Elmer Rice's claim in his autobiography that he wrote "some fifty full-length plays (about twenty of them unproduced); four novels, three of which have been published; a book about the theatre; an indeterminate number of short stories, one-act plays, articles, book reviews, motion pictures, radio and television scripts; and the present volume,"[1] only two of his plays have garnered lasting critical attention: *The Adding Machine* and *Street Scene*. Of these, the former still stands as a major contributor to the genre of American expressionism while the latter earned Rice his only Pulitzer Prize. The remainder of his work, though vast, has often been lumped together in examinations of Rice's dramaturgy rather than analyzed individually.

One play in particular is frequently neglected in examinations of Rice's oeuvre. *The Subway* (written 1923, performed 1929) is Rice's least-known American expressionist work. Though it followed closely behind *The Adding Machine* (1923) in conception, it was not produced until after *Street Scene* (1929). *The Subway*'s lowered status amongst his plays stems from its problematic production history and frequent comparison to Sophie Treadwell's *Machinal* (1928). Rice spoke little on the play, giving the entirety of its production history a mere three paragraphs in his autobiography, *Minority Report* (1963). Despite this, Rice believed the play to be a greater example of American expressionism than *The Adding Machine*. Further, he claimed that the comparisons to *Machinal* were not coincidental but in fact indicated a potential influence on Treadwell's play. Therefore, this study will present Rice's claim that *Machinal* was directly inspired by *The Subway* before analyzing the similarities between the works in order to suggest evidence of this direct influence on Treadwell's text.

There is a remarkably strong resemblance between *Machinal* and *The Subway*.

Both plays feature a nine-scene episodic structure which begins at the heroine's place of work. The plight of the female protagonist in both plays involves a desperate need to escape the trappings of a neglectful home life, an objectifying and mechanized workplace, and the maddeningly stifling commute via subway which connects the two. Like Sophie, Helen suffers a breakdown on the train to work, where she is subjected to mistreatment at the hands of her coworkers. The toll of the suffocating atmosphere is made evident through both protagonists' stilted, stream-of-consciousness monologues, which detail their hidden fears and desires. Even the texts of these monologues are similar, touching on religious love and the wandering hands of the subway passengers. Even the order and function of the scenes are uniquely similar. After a brief glimpse of her family, both narratives focus on her relationship with an artist, with particular emphasis on a scene in which the lovers meet in the dark and share a story. For Sophie, this is Eugene, with his tale of the subway-beast and the eternal beauty. For Helen, this is Mr. Roe, and his stories of the lands below the Rio Grande. Additionally, each heroine's only means of escaping her toxic environment is in this affair. However, it is this affair, ended by the artist's departure on business, which forces the heroine back into to society, and causes her subsequent downfall and eventual death by a machine. Both Sophie and Helen are interrogated for their actions, by an ethereal and corporeal jury respectively, and are killed.

These similarities between *The Subway* and *Machinal* were not lost on Rice, who came to believe that the textual parallels of the plays could not be coincidental. Believing the matter to be suspicious, Rice wrote to Arthur Hopkins, producer of both *Machinal* and *The Adding Machine*, on November 22, 1928. In the letter, Rice explained his suspicion; Treadwell, before the recent success of *Machinal*, worked as a play-reader for Broadway producers. In the six years before, Rice claimed to have sent *The Subway* to "every producer's office in New York," likely ensuring Treadwell read the play for her producer. While he did not enumerate on the similarities between the plays, he did call attention to the titles of both plays as an indication of the similarity, saying of *Machinal*: "Even the title, underscores the theme and emphasizes the mechanical background of the play in almost the same way that *The Subway* does."[2] He also mentioned that several of his friends, upon seeing *Machinal*, also thought the plays to be too similar for coincidence:

> Since then, numerous acquaintances who have read *The Subway*, have told me, of their own accord, that they too were struck by the numerous similarities between the two plays. So that I feel that I am not voicing the biased opinion of an author, jealous of his own rights, but am expressing the impartial judgement of a number of disinterested persons.[3]

He then explained that he did not believe Treadwell "deliberately borrowed from *The Subway*. But I do feel that the conclusion that she read the play and was influenced by it—consciously or unconsciously—is an inescapable one."[4] He reiterated that the situation seemed more accidental than intentional, removing the blame from Hopkins as well. However, Rice added that *The Subway* was about to be produced at the Cherry Lane Theatre and that, if it appeared that *Machinal* significantly damaged its opening, he would take action. He finished the letter by stating that he was anxious to avoid embarrassing or inconveniencing Hopkins and that, above all, he intended to preserve their friendship. Hopkins, however, never replied,[5] and it seems in response to this that, in January of 1929, Rice attempted to file an infringement suit against Treadwell with *The Billboard*, a theatre digest.[6] Rice's original suit cannot be found, but a response from M.P. Gudebrod of *The Billboard*'s editorial department is still extant. Gudebrod's letter does not enumerate a result of the suit, simply stating:

> I would appreciate an appointment with you, at your convenience, regarding your proposed suit for infringement against Miss Sophie Tread-well. I shall be glad to call at any time you set, and trust you can find time for this interview within the next few days.[7]

Oddly, the theatre digest's response is dated January 31, 1928. This must be an error as *Machinal* was not copyrighted until April 21 of that year[8] and Rice himself did not see it until November. Nonetheless, there is no evidence that the claim was ever followed up nor is there any information on the content of the interview. Allegedly, a program note was included for attendees of the Broadway performance of *The Subway*, which detailed Rice's previous attempts to have it published.[9] The play performed poorly, but Rice's mind was elsewhere, as *Street Scene* had just won the Pulitzer Prize in Drama. Rice subsequently abandoned any further attempts at pursuing his suspicions.

There is no further mention of Rice's proposed suit in his writings, whether in regard to its filing or its eventual dissolution. The author surely thought to take "such remedial measures as may seem advisable"[10] against feared financial damage from *Machinal*. He had already been burned by Broadway once; *The Adding Machine* famously drew in no money for its author. Further, none of the plays that followed *The Adding Machine* had been successful, and Rice had relied heavily on *The Subway*'s advance payments as he presented it to potential producers. *Machinal*'s popularity threatened to damage the profit margin he had fought to earn for six years, and an infringement claim must have seemed the logical solution. Unfortunately, there is also no record of why Rice dropped the intended suit, nor is there anything in Treadwell's surviving papers that indicate her awareness of Rice's concerns. It's likely that *The Subway*'s time on Broadway influenced the decision. In his letter to Hopkins, he promised that "if the damage appears to be negligible, I shall, of course, take no action."[11] With the move of *The Subway* to Broadway only twelve days after its opening, Rice may have believed the damage by *Machinal* was not as serious as he had anticipated and turned his attention back to the critically acclaimed *Street Scene*. Thus, by the time the Broadway production of *The Subway* failed, Rice simply decided it was not worth fighting for; having struggled for six years to produce the still-failing play and having other work perform significantly better, Rice likely thought he was cutting his losses by dropping the suit. Additionally, Rice may have feared spiting Hopkins, whose influence on Broadway as producer and director was far reaching. Rice had told Hopkins that he held "no obligation to Miss Treadwell, but I do to you," promising that he was "very anxious to avoid any action which would inconvenience or embarrass you"[12] and that he would not take action without first consulting Hopkins. In deciding not to pursue the claim, Rice may have sought to preserve a working relationship with Hopkins. The prevalence of infringement claims in the early twentieth century must also be taken into account when examining why it was dropped. In fact, Treadwell filed a plagiarism suit against famed actor John Barrymore years before her success with *Machinal*. In "Sophie Treadwell vs. John Barrymore: Playwrights, Plagiarism and Power in the Broadway Theatre of the 1920s," Dickey discusses this sudden upsurge of accusations:

> The decade of the 1920s in America saw an unprecedented number of punitive actions taken against theatrical plagiarists. These assertions included over twenty court suits, some against such well-known figures as Guy Bolton, George M. Cohan Channing Pollock, Sidney Howard, David Belasco, and R.C. Sherriff.[13]

This notorious upsurge coincided with a general suspicion of the writers who voiced their concerns. The press and public typically dismissed these artists as blackmailers looking for easy money. Plagiarism was simply too difficult to prove. This would explain why Rice ultimately decided against filing a suit; Rice risked much with this claim. Dickey states that most suits in the 1920s "came from unproduced dramatists who knew their suit would probably end any chance of their being accepted in the theatrical profession."[14] Rice had already made a national impact with the Broadway debut of *The Adding Machine* and risked damaging his future career on Broadway. More than that, *Street Scene* opened the same month he attempted the claim. By preparing such an accusation in the midst of a Broadway debut, he risked swaying public favor against him at a crucial moment in his career. Regardless of the reason, the matter was simply dropped without resolution. Rice continued working, albeit with hesitancy in reading new works, and Treadwell remained ignorant of the entire ordeal. With this in mind, *The Subway*'s noticeable lack of mention in Rice's later documents, particularly his autobiography, becomes clearer; he believed that *The Subway*'s failure and *Machinal*'s success were linked. Rice seemed convinced that *The Subway* was a lost cause, or even a poorly written show, glossing over it in subsequent mentions. Despite this, Rice never forgot this incident; in the following years, he instituted new personal rules to avoid unintentional influence. In one such response to an aspiring playwright's request for a reading, Rice informed him that "because of the frequency of literary coincidence and of the unfortunate misunderstandings which sometimes arise, I have had to make it an inflexible rule not to read the scripts of authors whom I do not know personally."[15] He replied similarly to another playwright, "because of the danger of plagiarism suits…,"[16] only relenting because the play's Russian subject matter interested him. This remark about the infringements could be a reference to the 1920s, a time known for frequent accounts of theatrical plagiarism, but may also have a personal significance.

> I think Miss Treadwell must have seen my play, *The Subway*, too. Or read it, rather, for it was not produced until sometime after *Machinal*. However,

it had been going the rounds of Broadway producers for years, and I actually sold it four times. Those were lean years for me, and the advance royalties enabled me and my family to live pleasantly in Paris and other delectable locales. During those years, Miss Treadwell was a play-reader for some Broadway producer – Crosby Gaige, I think – and while I do not suggest she was guilty of deliberate plagiarism, I assume that she could not help being influenced, unconsciously perhaps, by what she read.

He continues, explaining his letter to Hopkins, but omitting his attempt to file an infringement claim:

Anyhow, there are striking similarities between the two plays. I wrote to Arthur Hopkins, who produced *Machinal*, a discreet letter about it; but that man of silence, of course, never answered it.

He then describes the run of the show and subsequent Broadway failure:

The Subway was finally done by an amateur group at the Cherry Lane Theatre, which was off-Broadway even then (1929), though not so designated. Brady, intoxicated by the success of *Street Scene* (and perhaps by spiritous beverages) brought the production up to Broadway, where its amateurishness was fatally apparent. Not a very important bit of theatrical history, but I thought it might interest you.[17]

The letter concludes with Rice wishing Atkinson well in his retirement from the *New York Times*. Interestingly, this letter was written only one day after Atkinson's review of *Machinal*'s revival was published in the *Times*, suggesting the letter as a response to the revival and review. This implies that, years later, Rice still harbored ill feelings regarding *Machinal*'s success or in the very least indicates how deeply this experience affected him.

While scholarship on Treadwell's life has not validated Rice's claim that Treadwell worked as a Broadway play-reader, this fact is confirmed in multiple reviews of *Machinal*. One such review by Percy Hammond for the *Pittsburgh Press* states:

...and her [Treadwell's] favorite heroes are her husband, Mr. McGeehan, the acid sports critic of The New York Herald Tribune; Mr. Crosby Gaige, for whom she reads play manuscripts, and Mr. Arthur Hopkins, the producer of "Machinal."[18]

It is further confirmed in an article with *Vassar Miscellany News*, which gives Treadwell as Gaige's chief playreader.[19] It is unknown whether Treadwell read *The Subway*, but in a personal interview, Dr. Jerry Dickey, a leading scholar on Sophie Treadwell and her work, spoke of an interesting connection between Rice's play and a remark from a 1925 lecture. In it, Treadwell gives "a passing example of a situation that can spark a dramatist's imagination to write a play: riding a subway."[20] This seems to imply Treadwell's preoccupation with the setting, particularly for dramatic purposes. However, Dickey also conceded the possibility that "the idea was 'in the air' at the time."[21] While it cannot be established whether or not this points to a direct connection between the plays, it is a remarkably unique coincidence.

Rice does not expound upon the numerous similarities between the plays in his letter to Hopkins, but states that "they are numerous, especially in the earlier scenes of Machinal."[22] Thus, in order to answer the question of whether *Machinal* was inspired or at least influenced by *The Subway*, the content of both plays must be examined thoroughly. Through a comparison of the identical functions between corresponding scenes within the respective narratives, the validity of Rice's claim becomes more apparent.

In *The Subway*, the action commences with a scene at work, in which automaton-like workers carry in envelopes for Sophie to sort into cabinets. She seems to find a perfect means of escape from this mechanization through George, but her dreams are shattered when he announces his departure from New York. After his exit, Eugene and Hurst, while writing a piece on the company, ogle Sophie. The scene ends with their exit. *Machinal* begins similarly as Helen's place of work is established to be similarly mechanical, including instances of watching associates. Helen's co-workers gossip about her love life and the possibility of a marriage proposal from the boss, George H. Jones. When this is proven true, the proposal seems overwhelming to Helen; it could solve her financial burdens, but George himself is unappealing.

Both scenes propose an idealized marriage which could theoretically offer escape from suffocation, while also introducing the male character whose eventual relationship with the protagonist, while appearing as a solution to her predicament, will ultimately prove to be her demise. There are differences, too. In *The Subway* the idealized marriage and the male lead's entrance are separate incidents, George and Eugene respectively, while *Machinal* unites them into one event: George H. Jones' proposal. As well, Sophie is eager for the chance to marry George[23] and his announcement leaves her anxious. Helen, on the other hand, is left overwhelmed because of the marriage proposal itself, rather than the lack thereof.

The next scene in *The Subway* is Sophie's encounter in the subway, for which there is no equivalent scene in Treadwell's play. In *Machinal*, this corresponding attack is reduced, and moved into the first scene. In it, Helen does mention suffering an anxiety attack on the subway which causes her to be late for work. She defends herself meekly to her coworkers; "I thought I would faint! I had to get out in the air!"[24] This is distinctly similar to Sophie's own defense to her family; "Everything seemed like it was going around. I guess I must have fainted. Maybe it was the air, or I don't know what."[25] While Helen's attack is not shown onstage as Sophie's is in *The Subway*, it is just as devastating. She mentions it in her stilted monologue at the end of the episode, equivalating the thought of marrying George with the suffocation of the train. In both plays, the attack sets into motion the fear of society which compels both Sophie and Helen to seek escape from society.

The Subway's scene three is a glimpse into Sophie's home life. Her family does not interact with her directly, instead chattering incessantly while performing mindless tasks. This neglect gives Sophie only Eugene for conversation, developing the beginnings of their doomed affair through disjointed talk; "He talked so nice, too. He said-he said he'd come and see me some time."[26] *Machinal*'s scene two performs the same function, introducing the audience to the protagonist's neglectful family. Helen's mother ignores her, prescribing her own views on the young woman's life. At her mother's insistence, Helen agrees to marry George; "It's my hands got me a husband."[27] In both, the heroine's family, indirectly or directly, causes her to enter into the central relationship in the plot.

For Sophie, this relationship is the affair with Eugene, which is developed over the course of the rest of the play. Scene four establishes her guilt over the affair in a stilted, halting monologue. Following this is the scene in a movie theater, in which Eugene pressures Sophie into sex. Scenes three and four of *Machinal* provide the same ideas, but in reverse. In scene four, Helen voices a stilted, halting speech regarding her own guilt about having children with George. This occurs after the birth of their child, George having already attempted to pressure her into sex in scene three.

Here, the most impactful difference between the plays occurs; Eugene's counterpart in *Machinal* is divided between two men. While *The Subway*'s Eugene offers a means of escape from ordinary life through an affair, *Machinal*'s George offers escape through marriage, but Helen has the affair with Mr. Roe. Eugene is both the impetus for the action and the cause of Sophie's eventual downfall, while George is the impetus and Mr. Roe causes the downfall. This split allows George to remain consistently antagonistic over the course of the show, whereas Eugene does not initially appear as such. This difference impacts the remainder of both plays.

In scene six of *The Subway* and *Machinal*, the heroine is given a brief reprieve from society through an affair. This release comes through an extramarital relationship with an artist: Eugene and Mr. Roe, respectively. Further, this scene happens in near darkness onstage, with the artist recounting stories of foreign lands. For Eugene, this is the story of the subway-beast. For Roe, the discussion touches on Spain, the lands "below the Rio Grande," and Frisco. Sophie and Helen are both comforted by these stories, forgetting the outside world and its responsibilities for the length of the scene.

In both, the final scenes depict the downfall of the protagonist, as is frequent in expressionism. This downfall is the result of both the fear of returning to her former role in society and the betrayal of a lover. For Sophie, this is Eugene's job offer in Europe, which threatens to leave her a single mother. For Helen, this is the reality of living with George after her affair and her betrayal by Mr. Roe in court. Mr. Roe, like Eugene, leaves the heroine defenseless, open to scorn from her peers. In both, the oppressive society judges the heroine, scrutinizing her actions and ultimately condemning her as a failed mother. At the close of the play, she is killed by a machine.

Numerous linguistic similarities are also apparent. Both heroines are given to disjointed speeches which highlight their anxious, paranoiac train of thought. The greatest example of these occurs in scene four of both plays. In *The Subway*, Sophie expresses her anxiety over losing George and longs for an end to her loneliness. Her speech is fragmented and her thoughts at odds with each other. At the end, she prays to heaven, asking Jesus to love her:

> Oh, I'm so ashamed... so ashamed... Forgive me, dear Jesus... Comfort me... I love you so... Make me like you... make my heart as clean as yours... I'm all alone... Love me, dear Jesus... Take me to your heart... Love me... Love me... I'm so lonesome... so lonesome...[28]

Correspondingly, Helen's stilted monologue in *Machinal*'s scene four seems almost an answer to Sophie's; similarly disjointed and anxious, it confronts the belief of God as love instead of embracing it: "everybody loves God—they've got to—got to—got to love God—God is love—even if he's bad they got to love him..."[29] These staccato speeches, peppered with fretful anxiety, provide the same function for their respective protagonists, a means of expressing thought in a suffocating environment. The halting pace reflects a disjointed mindset, which both protagonists share.

Further, these linguistic similarities even carry over into word usage and topic. In some cases, these staccato monologues are almost identical. In the best example of this, both plays have their heroine speak of the ominous dread which accompanies riding the subway. In her first monologue in *Machinal*, Helen speaks aloud her fears of men touching her while riding the train:

> Fat hands— flabby hands— don't touch me— please— fat hands are never weary— please don't... don't touch me— please— no— can't— must— somebody— something— no rest— must rest— no rest— must rest— no rest— late today— yesterday— before— late— subway— air— pressing— bodies pressing— bodies – trembling...[30]

Here, the subway is given as a place of oppression, where the stifling air crowds its passengers. This claustrophobia is shared in Sophie. In *The Subway*'s scene four, Sophie voices her own fears:

> Oh, dear Jesus, why do you make me ride in the subway? ... I hate it, hate it, hate it ... They put their hands on you ... all over you ... But I'm too scared to say anything ... I don't know what to say ... Oh, my sweet Jesus, don't let them touch me like that[31]

In both monologues, the heroine specifically mentions the touching of strangers on the subway. In scene two of *Machinal*, Helen even tells her mother her fear of dying on the train. The subway's specific usage within these plays is significant, indicating that both works utilize the same tool for the same purpose; the subway becomes a focal point of unconscious fear, which plagues both Sophie and Helen.

The subway in both plays is a symbol not only for the mechanization of society, but for the ambivalence of the people to this mechanization. Both heroines specifically address their horror at the willingness of people to pack themselves so tightly onto the train, mentioning the pressing of bodies against them. In *The Subway*, each stop is a battlefield of passengers forcing themselves through each other; "The faces on the platform grow tense, muscles taut with the anticipation of battle. The readers lower their newspapers. Sophie closes her book. Her lips are drawn, her eyes a little terrified."[32] Helen doesn't directly describe the passengers of the subway but does mention their proximity to her; "All those bodies pressing."[33] These passengers, however, do not seem to notice. In *The Subway*, they are merely "staring vacuously, imbecilely."[34] The subway is a necessary evil and its riders have become desensitized to its barbarity.

The usage of a female protagonist is also significant. *The Subway* and *Machinal* are two of only three major expressionist works with a female lead. This fact in itself creates a similarity between the works and is highlighted when considering the third, *The Verge*, holds almost nothing else in common with them. The mechanical themes of *The Subway* and *Machinal* are completely absent in *The Verge*, which in fact deals with the reverse in botany and biology. Further, the former two plays deal primarily with a protagonist forcibly isolated from society and longing to regress to a simpler time. *The Verge*'s Claire Archer is isolated from her peers, but only through her own desire to press forward into abstraction and "the beyond." The similarities between *The Subway* and *Machinal* are much more evident when considering the third female-driven expressionist play.[35]

A final note worth mentioning is the similarity in title. Both *Machinal* and *The Subway* as titles are evocative of the mechanical aspects of their plays, underscoring their central themes. While this may seem coincidental, few other American expressionist plays, save Rice's *The Adding Machine*, represented their mechanical subject matter directly in their title. In fact, by and large, most plays of the genre dealt with the biological in their title – Susan Glaspell's *The Verge*; Eugene O'Neill's *The Emperor Jones* and *The Hairy Ape*; George S. Kaufman and Marc Connelly's *Beggar on Horseback*; and John Howard Lawson's *Roger Bloomer*.[36]

This, however, speaks to a deeper connection. While the mechanization of society is a distinct hallmark of American expressionism, it rarely becomes the overarching theme of the piece. In both *Machinal* and *The Subway*, a criticism of America's mechanically-obsessed culture is inseparable from the plot. The death of the heroine at the hands of a machine is not insignificant; both women seek escape into a pastoral, idyllic world through their respective artists, but are forced to face a masculine-driven, mechanical society. In few other plays are the protagonists persecuted directly by the mechanical nature of society. For example, *The Hairy Ape*'s Yank is accosted by automaton-like people in multiple scenes; the laughs of the other sailors in scene four have "*a brazen, metallic quality as if their throats were phonograph horns*"[37] while the businessmen of scene five exhibit "*something of the relentless horror of Frankensteins in their detached, mechanical unawareness.*"[38] Yank believes himself to be part of this pure, mechanized society, but in reality this mechanization is nothing more than a facet of a larger capitalist system. O'Neill, cynical in his views of labor, utilizes mechanization as a tool of the larger corporate powers at work, through which Yank is persecuted. Similarly, *Beggar on*

Horseback deals with wealth from industry than with the technology itself. In both *The Subway* and *Machinal*, however, this theme of mechanization is tied more closely to masculinity than capitalism. This mechanical masculinity, unique within the genre, centers the expressionist journey on the heroine's femininity through direct and overwhelming opposition to it.

Not all of *Machinal* is reminiscent of *The Subway*. In fact, it is the aspects of the play that resemble the Snyder trial that differentiate it from Rice's work; the latter half of *Machinal* is a direct reference to the trial and is, admittedly, where the similarities to *The Subway* begin to weaken. Even Rice conceded that the strongest indicators of influence occurred in the first half; "I shall not at this time enumerate all the points of similarity, but I assure you that they are numerous, especially in the earlier scenes of *Machinal*."[39] This departure begins in scene seven, where the impact of the male character split becomes more apparent.

While Sophie initially turns to despair and refuses to respond to Eugene's impending abandonment, Helen turns on her husband and kills him. These both end in the protagonist judged and sentenced, but both occur in different ways. During these last three scenes, *Machinal* takes the form of a literal courtroom drama while *The Subway* becomes a figurative one. This split is important, however, as it indicates a shift in influence on Treadwell's part. While the first six scenes heavily resemble *The Subway*, the last three scenes bear a less noticeable similarity, with *Machinal* more closely resembling the Ruth Snyder trial. The scenes which resemble *The Subway* set the stage for those which resemble the trial, effectively allowing the trial to take place and lending credit to the idea that its inspiration is shared in both. *The Subway*'s presence as a setup for the trial within the play furthers this idea; the trial remains the central concept of *Machinal*. This strengthens the argument for *Machinal*'s unintended inspiration; when Treadwell became inspired to write a play to defend Ruth Snyder, she likely drew upon ideas she believed to be her own, specifically ideas from *The Subway*, in order to set it into motion.

In light of Rice's unfiled claim, *The Subway* gains new prominence as an influential factor on a staple of the American expressionist theatre, *Machinal*. Their shared themes, usages of expressionism, and plot lines are too coincidental and indicate Treadwell's prior familiarity with the script. These similarities were evident even to theatre-goers and critics at the time, contributing to *The Subway*'s failed opening and its subsequent status as a footnote within the influential genre. As well, historical evidence points to Treadwell's role as a playreader during the six years Rice attempted to have *The Subway* produced. With this in mind, Machinal's inspiration by The Subway becomes both apparent and probable.

---

[1] Elmer Rice, *Minority Report: An Autobiography*, (New York: Simon and Schuster, 1963), 470.

[2] Ibid.

[3] Ibid.

[4] Ibid.

[5] Letter to Brooks Atkinson, "' '--Miscellaneous' 1936-1965," 9 April 1960, E76-154 to E76-215, Box 46, Folder 3, Harry Ransom Humanities Research Center, University of Texas, Austin, Texas.

[6] It is important to keep in mind that copyright law was difficult to prove in court during this era. Rice's attempt to file a claim through a theatre digest such as *The Billboard* is more akin to filing a grievance within the theatrical community than a modern copyright infringement suit.

[7] Letter from M.P. Gudebrod, "Business Correspondence, *The Subway*," 31 January 1928, B58-654 to B58-718, Box 75, Folder 5, Harry Ransom Humanities Research Center, University of Texas, Austin, Texas.

[8] Dickey, "The Expressionist Moment," 72.

[9] From the Reviews of the Subway, "Business Correspondence, *The Subway*," B58-654 to B58-718, Box 75, Folder 5, Harry Ransom Humanities Research Center, University of Texas, Austin, Texas.

[10] Letter to Arthur Hopkins, "Business Correspondence, *The Subway*," 22 November 1928, B58-654 to B58-718, Box 75, Folder 5, Harry Ransom Humanities Research Center, University of Texas, Austin, Texas.

[11] Ibid.

[12] Ibid.

[13] Dickey, "Sophie Treadwell vs. John Barrymore," 68.

[14] Ibid., 75.

[15] Letter to Mr. Sprague, "Plays Read," 3 March 1933, B54-220 to B54-243, Box 67, Folder 6, Harry Ransom Humanities Research Center, University of Texas, Austin, Texas.

[16] Letter to Mr. Makaroff, "Plays Read," 13 September 1932, B54-220 to B54-243, Box 67, Folder 6, Harry Ransom Humanities Research Center, University of Texas, Austin, Texas.

[17] Letter to Brooks Atkinson, "' '--Miscellaneous' 1936-1965," 9 April 1960, E76-154 to E76-215, Box 46, Folder 3, Harry Ransom Humanities Research Center, University of Texas, Austin, Texas.

[18] Hammond, "The Theater – 'Machinal' Gratifying,'" 64.

[19] "Community Theatre Production Attracts First Nighters," *Vassar Miscellany News* 8.3, 6 October 1928, 1.

[20] Jerry Dickey, in discussion with the author. February 2019.

[21] Ibid.

[22] Letter to Arthur Hopkins, "Business Correspondence, *The Subway*," 22 November 1928, B58-654 to B58-718, Box 75, Folder 5, Harry Ransom Humanities Research Center, University of Texas, Austin, Texas.

[23] The usage of the name George for the idealized partner in the first scene of both plays could be considered a notable similarity; due to its lack of significance on the plot, this is more likely coincidence, however.

[24] Treadwell, *Machinal*, 6.

[25] Rice, *The Subway*, 44.

[26] Ibid.

[27] Treadwell, *Machinal*, 20.

[28] Ibid., 55-6.

[29] Treadwell, *Machinal*, 30.

[30] Ibid., 12.

[31] Rice, *The Subway*, 52.

[32] Ibid., 28.

[33] Treadwell, *Machinal*, 6.

[34] Rice, *The Subway*, 27.

[35] In regard to minor American expressionist plays, Hungarian-American playwright Francis Faragoh's *Pinwheel* also deals with a young, female office worker who, after developing an affair, kills her lover. For more information on how this play compares to *Machinal*, *The Subway*, and Maurine Watkins' *Chicago*, please refer to Jerry Dickey's article, "Working Women and Violence in Jazz Era American Drama."

[36] An exception could be argued for Hungarian-American playwright Lajos Egri's *Rapid Transit*, a little known 1927 expressionist play which deals with the rapidity of human life in the industrial age. This play, however, is starkly different from both *The Subway* and *Machinal*, imagining the compression of its characters' entire lives into the span of 24 hours.

[37] Eugene O'Neill, *The Hairy Ape*, (New York: The Modern Library, 1949), 210.

[38] Ibid., 225.

[39] Letter to Arthur Hopkins, "Business Correspondence, *The Subway*," 22 November 1928, B58-654 to B58-718, Box 75, Folder 5, Harry Ransom Humanities Research Center, University of Texas, Austin, Texas.

(RE)NEGOTIATING DEMOCRACY AND THEATRE: HALLIE FLANAGAN DAVIS' INTEGRATION OF ANTIQUITY IN THE FEDERAL THEATRE PROJECT

Shelby Lunderman
University of Washington, Seattle

Hallie Flanagan Davis, often remembered for running the short-lived yet highly-influential Federal Theatre Project (FTP), became the first woman awarded the prestigious Guggenheim Fellowship in 1926. For her fellowship, Flanagan Davis spent twelve months studying European models of theatrical production, traveling to France, Austria, Germany, England, Ireland, Scandinavia, Russia, Italy, Hungary, and Czechoslovakia from July 1926-July 1927. She sought to understand the "traditional European methods of production of the plays of classic artist, and [...] new developments along the lines of play writing, scenic design, lighting, acting, and direction, as seen in the great theatres, both professional and experimental...."[1] This research undoubtedly impacted Flanagan Davis' artistic endeavors, as seen in her later writings, such as her memoir, *Arena,* which recounted her time with the FTP:

> It convinced me that all of these so-called new forms had ancient proto-types, that rigid adherence to any one school or cult hampered the theatre, and that every play dictated its own terms as to form of acting and as to de-sign. It also proved to me that any person working in the field of the thea-tre should learn as much as he possibly could of history, literature, religion, language, art, economics, science, in order that each play he did might be informed from the past and integrated in the present.[2]

For her, avant-garde theatre, even in its attempt to forge new paths, used the bricks of the past. Beyond that, however, Flanagan Davis knew she personally needed to excavate the ruins of theatre's history now more than ever to understand her present theatrical journey.

Just seven years later, in 1934, she decided to expand upon her comparative global theatre grand tour. Along with her husband, Vassar ancient Greek professor Philip Davis, Flanagan Davis traveled to Italy, Africa, Sicily, and Greece. While in Greece, the two were drawn to the ruins of antiquity, going so far as to translate inscriptions on the ruins they explored. A third century BCE Apollonian shrine at theatre at Delos particularly caught their eye for its engraved descriptions of ancient theatrical activity.[3] Flanagan Davis, grappling with this experience of antiquity, recounted, "What festivals, processionals, what strange goings-on, long lost in antiquity, in the great theatre where five thousand people once filled the marble seats?"[4] Flanagan Davis was fascinated with the ancient past, particularly ancient Greece's government-funded theatre and sought to investigate why the Greeks saw theatre as fundamental to preserving their democracy. She continued, "These shows had cost money. Sometimes the inscriptions recorded comparatively small amounts... Sometimes expenditures were for enormous hauls of marble or of lumber... Whatever had gone on had evidently been worth paying for out of government money, for this theatre had been erected and the play put on at the expense of the government."[5] Exploring the core relationship between theatre and government—specifically democracy—clearly captivated her. As an American in the post-Great War United States, she sought to understand how theatre funding was both rationalized and seen as fundamental to a core exploration of democratic ideals. Years later in her 1940 FTP memoir, *Arena*, she wrote, "After Greece almost any other country would be theatrically anti-climactic."[6] This seemingly innocent comment about her trip does not just reveal that she held the memories of Greece close to her heart. More deeply, the comment exposes how profoundly Flanagan Davis internalized her observations about the relationship between democracy and theatre, which paved the way for the climax of her own theatrical career: The Federal Theatre Project.

Flanagan Davis' interest in antiquity supplied her with an idealistic vision re-garding the relationship between theatre and democracy that extended beyond any given play's ability to comment on current events. She believed that theatre could be a fundamental part of a functional democracy, supported and funded by the state, yet free to critique it when necessary. Despite Flanagan Davis' deep interest in participation with this imagined past to better her country's flailing present, Flanagan Davis' deployment of antiquity was a key factor in the program's downfall. Upon deeper inspection, the theatre and the state's relationship have always been anything but idealistic.

The FTP was one of the five arts relief programs within the Federal Project Number One (FPNO), a subset of the Works Progress Administration (WPA). [7] Created by Franklin D. Roosevelt in 1935, the WPA, FPNO, and FTP were all a part of New Deal legislation that attempted to create jobs for starving, unemployed, and often homeless Americans during the Great Depression.[8] Specifically, the FTP sought to create jobs for unemployed theatre artists—actors, directors, designers, playwrights, composers/lyricists, and more—through the production of new and established plays. Harry Hopkins, the director of the WPA and FPNO, sought out Hallie Flanagan Davis, then currently employed at Vassar College, to design and head the new program. Hopkins, aware of her Guggenheim research, wanted Flanagan Davis to establish a national theatre that focused on relief, but gave her freedom in the design and implementation of the program.[9] She, according to Bonnie Nelson Schwartz in *Voices from the Federal Theatre Project,* "was convinced that such a project, though conceived as a source of economic relief, was obliged to establish and maintain high artistic standards."[10] This artistic endeavor, however, could not be accomplished through one single action or mandate.

Flanagan Davis recognized that relief roll actors did not equal amateur or un-skilled theatre-makers. As expressed in a recounted conversation with Hopkins, she knew that many were seasoned artists, unemployed not only because of the Great Depression but also due to the emerging competition from cinema and radio.[11] The large, talented labor force allowed Flanagan Davis to dream of a program larger than those she researched across the globe.

Flanagan Davis thus set out to create a new standard of national theatre unparal-leled by those she had researched around the world. Her deviation from her interna-tional research first propelled her to design a decentralized theatre, "creating productions not just in New York but in every major city and region of the coun-try."[12] Instead of having a singular national theatre housed in one central building, such as the Comédie-Française in France, Flanagan Davis decided to use existing theatres around the country and repurpose spaces for theatrical performance outside the typical theatre-centric cities such as New York. This would not only allow the average U.S. citizen to see theatre, but to also participate in the relief rolls, ultimately cultivating a nation of spectators and theatre artists. By the end of the first year of the programs operation in 1935, the FTP was operating in 40 cities of 22 states with over 6000 workers.[13] Furthermore, they produced a wide variety of classical plays, theatre of youth, theatre of the dance, new American plays, Negro theatre, research and experimentation, radio, Vaudeville, and more in a concerted effort to appeal to the masses, work towards the FTP's mission, and create quality art.[14]

According to Flanagan Davis, a decentralized national theatre would ideally lead to a better functioning democracy. Separate from the employment of thousands on the relief rolls, she wanted, "to produce plays that were not mere entertainments but artworks relevant to the social and political problems of the day."[15] Flanagan Davis wanted accessible theatre in every pocket of the U.S. to comment on current events and the socio-political issues plaguing the residents of the country to activate their understanding and participation.. She firmly believed that such theatre would lead to a better country, an undoubtedly necessary vision amidst the Great Depression. In *Arena,* she wrote that theatre, "is a necessity because in order to make democracy work the people must increasingly participate; they can't participate unless they understand; and the theatre is one of the great mediums of understanding."[16] These comments, when linked to her known travels and research throughout antiquity, reveal her entrenched motivation for turning to theatre during a tumultuous time for the United States. For Flanagan Davis, history had proven that theatre was fundamental to democracy.

Despite the success of the day-to-day operations, however, Flanagan Davis still had to defend the funding of theatre by the government. Despite her firm belief that theatre played a vital role in a healthy democracy, she was often forced to legitimize the FTP through its production of canonical playwrights, including, as she stated in front of Congress, "Euripides, Plautus, Marlowe, Shakespeare, Beaumont, and Fletcher, Lope de Vega, Moliere, Sheridan, Labiche, Ibsen, Wilde, Shaw and O'Neill."[17] Although the list of produced playwrights is more expansive than this one here, Flanagan Davis knew that respected playwrights would earn respect for the program.[18] Furthermore, she distinguished, in briefs delivered to Congress, that the playwrights were "important dramatists both classical and modern."[19] This categorization worked twofold: to show that the FTP maintained contemporary relevance through its constant work with new, modern playwrights that were tackling current issues and to legitimize the program through its associations with the established, tested authority of the classical. By often explaining that they were producing plays by Aristophanes, Euripides, etc., Flanagan Davis attached the FTP to a millenniums-old tradition of Greek theatre that functioned with the original and coveted democracy.

Flanagan Davis was particularly attracted to the economic structure of the Greek theatre, where money was seemingly no object. The city funded the building of theatres, festivals, and productions, chorus actors from the military were paid fees, and rich choregos pitched in to fund their own productions of promising playwrights. This history, known to Flanagan Davis due to her studies and travel, found its way into her rationale of the FTP. Although her knowledge of Greek theatre and how it functioned in society ran further and deeper than this simplification, she repetitively invoked this imagined past about how theatre funding worked in Athens. Through this equation, she hoped that she could find support in her contemporaneous democracy. If the Greeks so valued theatre as a part of their democracy that they funded it, and the United States wanted to build a democracy like the Greeks in the face of the prevailing economic hardships and returning political turmoil, then Americans needed theatre.

She recognized that the public and government, beyond Hopkins, must perceive theatre as vital to democracy in order to maintain the FTP's funding. In a written brief delivered to Congress in 1938, Flanagan Davis' attempt to rationalize government funds for theatre was apparent. Flanagan Davis wrote, "Athens believed that plays were worth paying for out of public money; [and that] today, France, Germany, Norway, Sweden, Denmark, Russia, Italy, and practically all other civilized countries appropriate money for the theatre."[20] Although the FTP had already been operating for three years by the time this brief was delivered, Flanagan Davis used antiquity divisively. Aside from establishing the cultural currency of theatre in Athens, as discussed above, she turned to the other countries that she believed already copied the Greek belief that theatre should be funded. Through this, she proposed that the United States is perhaps behind its civilized counterparts. Flanagan Davis, once again, inscribed this imagined past by asking Congress to remember Athens in hopes that they would value and fund theatre like the great leaders of democracy before them had.

Within the FTP itself, Flanagan Davis moved more meticulously when it came to reinscribing antiquity. The productions of Greek and Roman plays and the constant attempt to inscribe the Greek model of theatrical production were just a few ways in which the program participated in the imagined past. The program's engagement with antiquity, however, beyond these two components, was a considerable component of the FTP as a whole. Flanagan Davis wrote, "Considerations of dance, of choric speech, of drama of the past produced for a modern audience, and above all, of the necessity for any living theatre to be of its own time and country, had a profound effect on such apparently unrelated Federal Theatre productions as *Power, Murder in the Cathedral, One-Third of a Nation,* and *America Sings.*"[21] She sought to understand, teach, and implement the structure of Greek theatre, instead of just employing in the works of its originally intended playwrights. The plays listed above, all of which discuss current events, engaged with antiquity in a deeper way. Like Aeschylus, Sophocles, Euripides, and Aristophanes, the playwrights of the FTP sought to comment on their contemporaneous socio-political moment through both direct and in-direct settings, characters, and dialogue. The plays were intended to critique the state, and—like those preformed at the Acropolis—critique the very members potentially sitting in the audience. Undoubtedly informed by her conclusions from her Guggenheim Fellowship research, Flanagan Davis wanted these modern dramas to recognize their ancient past through an onstage negotiation of theatrical critique of democracy. One could not see the antiquity onstage in columns or listed in the programs, but if audiences sliced the productions open, they would have bled antiquity beloved by Hallie Flanagan.

Despite this dynamic use of antiquity to bring authority to FTP and ensure its survival, the plan ultimately backfired. The FTP was known for its left-leaning sentiments, and as fears of Communism grew throughout the country, the program was increasingly placed in the spotlight.

By 1938, the Dies Committee, later referred to as the House Un-American Activities Committee (HUAC), launched a full-fledge investigation into the program for its ties to communism and spreading the communist message across the U.S. The Committee accused the FTP of actively producing plays in every major city in the country that spouted communist messages in attempt to recruit new Communist Party members. *Revolt of the Beavers,* for example, got the program in hot water after copies of Brook Atkinson's review of landed on the desk of the senators. The children's play, which he called "Marxism-a-la-Mother Goose", taught children about workers' rights through a cheery musical with roller-skating beavers. The Dies Committee also believed that the FTP was riddled with members of the Communist Party, an assumption rooted in an anti-theatrical hysteria that lived long into the 1960s.

In December of the investigation, they subpoenaed Flanagan Davis to interrogate her about the structure of the program, the rationale behind certain plays' productions, and more. In one specific exchange with Congressman Starnes Flanagan Davis fought back against assertions that certain playwrights had communist ties:

MR. STARNES: You are quoting from this Marlowe. Is he a Communist?

MRS. FLANAGAN: I am very sorry. I was quoting from Christopher Marlowe.

MR. STARNES: Tell us who Marlowe is, so we can get the proper reference, because that is all that we want to do.

MRS. FLANAGAN: Put in the record that he was the greatest dramatist in the period immediately preceding Shakespeare.

MR. STARNES: Put that in the record because the charge has been made that this article of yours is entirely Communistic, and we want to help you.

MRS. FLANAGAN: Thank you. That statement will go in the record.

MR. STARNES: Of course, we had what some people call 'Communists' back in the days of the Greek theater.

MRS. FLANAGAN: Quite true.

MR. STARNES: And I believe Mr. Euripides was guilty of teaching class-consciousness also, wasn't he?

MRS. FLANAGAN: I believe that was alleged against all of the Greek dramatists.

MR. STARNES: So we cannot say when it began.[22]

This exchange reveals a deeply anti-theatrical sentiment within the committee. The major issue, however, is that labeling Euripides and Marlowe as communists espousing class-consciousness is anachronistic at best. Flanagan Davis recognized the Congressman's deep-rooted anti-theatrical sentiment which resulted in false logic. When she jokingly pokes back at him, however, Starnes only re-asserts his views: theatre was always communist and always will be. Although Flanagan Davis had often turned to antiquity to rationalize the funding of the FTP, the imagined past, here, failed her. Congress had brought in antiquity as well, but for a completely different purpose. They chose to remember Euripides—who was disliked by the Greeks—for his subversion against the state and anachronistically implied that theatre has always focused on class-consciousness and Marxism.

Neither the production of Greek playwrights, inscribing the mythically great Athens, nor filling plays with the essence of Greek theatre led to the demise of the FTP, however. After Flanagan Davis' testimony, however, as well as years of accusations and an all-out witch hunt, a relief bill was passed in 1939, which stripped FTP of its funding. With Congress' overwhelming support of 373 votes to 21 in favor of the bill, social acceptance of the FTP and federally funded theatre waned as well.[23] Beyond the reasoning that the FTP attempted to spread communist ideals, Senator John Parnell Thomas, serving member of the Dies Committee, reasoned "that the Federal Theatre Project not only [was] serving as a branch of the communist organization but... also one more link in the vast and unparalleled New Deal propaganda machine."[24] The argument that the Committee's distaste for New Deal legislation propelled the shutdown is misguided and incomplete for a multitude of reasons. In the beginning years of his political career, Martin Dies, Jr. supported much of the New Deal since it provided economic relief to areas such as his rural Texas district and the Dies Committee recognized the benefits of many other FPNO projects throughout their hearings. There had to be something deeper at the root of their reasoning, something based in a deep distaste for theatre and theatre's relationship to democracy, which is revealed in their attack on Greek playwrights.

Although she often only inscribed a baseline understanding of Athens and Greek theatre to rationalize the funding of the FTP, Flanagan Davis knew and recognized the darker side of Greece's theatrical history. She saw the parallels as they unfolded in her own life and recounted the harsh realities in her memoir. In her detailed account about *One-Third of a Nation*, she recognized why the 1938 FTP original living newspaper about delinquency, slums, and the rising housing crisis was controversial.[25] The play called out powerful landlords and wealthy families for their apathy towards the low and middle classes.[26] She recalls, *"One-Third of a Nation, like any powerful play on a controversial subject, made enemies as well as friends. There is nothing new about this situation. Aristophanes was accused of treason because The Babylonians, paid for out of the government money, criticized Athen's foreign policy...."*[27] Here, Flanagan Davis remembers a more detailed history not promoted in her briefs or her speeches. This account is not one of convenience, but rather a parallel in the conflict between the state and the theatre, one that she had previously left out in her defense of government funding of the FTP. In this moment, Flanagan Davis also remembers her time at the Apollonian shrine. She recalled, "A replica of one of these inscriptions, which started with the phrase—'We let out these works on the vote of the people'—was displayed for four years on the wall of the Washington office of the Federal Theatre—a theatre the contracts for which, twenty-two centuries later, were also let out according to the dictates of democracy."[28] Although she moved on quickly from this rather introspective moment in her memoir, Flanagan Davis sees that the very democracy she inscribed to fund her theatre became the very tool with which Congress defunded the FTP.

To single-handedly point to the antiquity within the Federal Theatre Project would be an impossible feat. For Flanagan Davis, it idealistically manifested boldly through certain productions and in the cracks and crevices of others. More importantly, however, the antiquity of the FTP was an inscription of a way of life twenty-two centuries old. The Greek theatre model offered a way to reconsider how theatre can function in and around the state, an apparatus of theatre-making where Flanagan Davis believed some of the greatest plays were ever written. To dream of recreating such brilliant work in the U.S. is highly commendable. She believed in the unemployed artists of the Great Depression, and in this country's most distraught moment, she turned to what she believed to be the most functioning model of government-funded theatre. Ultimately, however, the ruins of the very past she pushed others to remember had too many parallels for its own good, leading to the demise of the FTP and quashing the idea of a potential U.S. national theatre in the future.

---

[1] "Hallie Flanagan Davis," John Simon Guggenheim Memorial Foundation, accessed March 9, 2017, http://www.gf.org/fellows/all-fellows/hallie-flanagan-davis/.

[2] Hallie Flanagan, *Arena: The History of the Federal Theatre* (New York: Duell, Sloan and Pearce, 1940), 4.

[3] There are three Apollonian shrines at Delos, and its unknown which one she is referencing in this moment.

[4] Ibid., 5.

[5] Ibid..

[6] Ibid., 6.

[7] William Young, and Nancy Young, *The Great Depression in America: A Cultural Encyclopedia, Volume 2* (Westport, CT: Greenwood Publishing Group, 2007), 171.

[8] Ibid., 171.

[9] Hallie Flanagan, *Arena*, 7-9.

[10] Bonnie Nelson Schwartz, *Voices from the Federal Theatre Project* (University of Wisconsin Press, 2003), xii.

[11] Ibid., 9.

[12] Ibid., xii.

[13] Hallie Flanagan, United States, House of Representations, Committee on Patents, *Brief Delivered by Hallie Flanagan* (Washington D.C., 1938).

[14] Ibid. Pulled from the brief, these subsets are just a few of the many known departments that operated with the Federal Theatre Project. The importance of these, however, is that they were used to defend the FTP against accusations of Communist activity and show the important work that the program was doing for multiple demographics.

[15] Bonnie Nelson Schwartz, *Voices from the Federal Theatre Project,* xii.

[16] Hallie Flanagan, *Arena,* 372.

[17] *Hearings before the House Committee on Un-American Activities, 1938–1968* (New York: The Viking Press, 1971), 24–25.

[18] Hallie Flanagan, *Arena,* 375-436. The appendix, "Production Record and Financial Statement," located in Flanagan's *Arena,* contains a concise list of plays produced. The list however is now conclusive, as it does not include every production and/or adaptation from smaller cities and rural productions.

[19] Ibid., 221.

[20] Flanagan, *Brief Delivered by Hallie Flanagan.*

[21] Hallie Flanagan, *Arena,* 6.

[22] *Hearings before the House Committee on Un-American Activities,* 24–25.

[23] Bonnie Schwartz Nelson, *Voices from the Federal Theatre Project,* xviii.

[24] *The New York Times*, July 27, 1938, p. 19 J. Parnell Thomas.

[25] Arthur Arent, et al. *Federal Theatre Plays* (New York: Random House, 1938).

[26] Hallie Flanagan, *Arena,* 216-220.

[27] Ibid., 220.

[28] Ibid., 5-6.

A MOTHER'S IMAGE: PORTRAITS OF ELLEN TERRY BY EDWARD GORDON CRAIG

Aubrey Helene Neumann
The Ohio State University

INTRODUCTION: A PRODUCTIVE STRIKE

Edward Gordon Craig (1872-1966) had a flair for self-deprecation. In *Woodcuts and Some Words* (1924), Craig refers to the period from 1898 to 1900 as his "strike for lower wages."[1] After leaving a profitable acting position but before embarking on a career in design and theory, Craig found himself at a loss. Yet this droll reference fails to capture the great productivity Craig achieved during this time period. In 1899 alone Craig designed and engraved 87 woodcuts, released four issues of his journal *The Page*, and published the book *Henry Irving, Ellen Terry, etc.*[2] Not only was he very prolific during this time, but Craig's experiments in woodblock printing and journal editing also paved the way for his later design innovations and directorial theories.[3]

Motivated by both artistic and financial need, Craig often used his mother's image to secure an audience for his work. The actress Ellen Terry (1847-1928) had gained renown acting opposite Henry Irving at the Lyceum Theatre, causing her name and image to be in high demand. Fans flocked to see her perform, authors wrote books about her, and advertisers sought her endorsement. Whereas photographs and advertisements depict Terry as an object of sexual desire, albeit in her declining years, Craig's portraits' reveal another story. Growing up amidst an oft-touring theatre company with a revolving door of father figures, Terry was one of few constants in Craig's young life. Her connections secured his early acting career, she financed his first foray into directing and designing, and her paychecks often went towards Craig's own children when he was unwilling or unable to support them. The popular portraits depicting Terry as a sexual object, subservient flirt, and/or aging actress, undermined the strength Craig had come to rely on over the years, or so his portraits suggest. From 1898 to 1900, Craig repeatedly portrayed his mother as a determined, strong woman. His woodblock portraits desexualize his mother's image, instead emphasizing her vitality and agency.

Though scholars like Peter Holland have stressed the import of Craig's later engravings, these early woodblock prints remain largely overlooked.[4] Closer analysis reveals not only the financial straits and artistic exploration that led to Craig's later innovations, but also Craig's complex relationship with his mother's image. Craig appropriates Terry's image for his own financial gain while at the same time attempting to reinstill her agency. This article provides a historical counterpoint to current discussions of the female image as well as insight into the personal relationship between a groundbreaking theatre artist...and his mother.

WOODBLOCK PRINTING: A LOW-COST REHEARSAL

The year 1898 found Craig at a crossroads both personally and professionally. Though he had begun acting alongside his mother in Henry Irving's Lyceum company in 1889, an imprudent marriage to May Gibson in 1893 permanently disrupted his career. Craig almost immediately regretted this union, recalling, "[Henry Irving] offered me *parts* and *glory* and *money*...but I needed a woman. In consequence I married, which was the wrong thing to do."[5] As Craig hinted, the marriage prevented him from traveling abroad with Irving and the rest of the Lyceum company in the summer of 1893. Instead, Craig accepted larger roles with lesser-acclaimed touring companies, which allowed him to stay in England. When Craig asked to rejoin the Lyceum company in 1896, both Terry and Irving declined, believing that Craig would benefit from more time away from the Lyceum where he was "spoiled."[6] Terry later relented, and Craig continued to act in occasional Lyceum productions, but his apprenticeship with Irving had effectively ceased.

Craig's ill-advised marriage merely hastened the end of his acting career. Despite early promise, Craig soon realized that he had neither the talent nor the inclination to continue as an actor. He later described his decision to leave acting as follows:

> But when I watched [Henry Irving] in the last act of "The Lyons Mail" and in "The Bells," I felt that beyond that there was no going, and I told myself that I could either be content for the rest of my life to follow Irving and become a feeble imitation of him, or discover who I was and be that. So I made my choice, and I turned my back on Irving for many a year...[7]

Refusing to continue in Irving's shadow, Craig sought out other possibilities. He had already begun to develop new ideas as to the true nature of theatre – ideas that were very much at odds with the style of the Lyceum company. An avid reader, Craig consulted Goethe, Nietzche, Ruskin and Tolstoy. According to biographer Denis Bablet, Craig combined and reinterpreted their theories to develop his own set of ideas regarding the futility of conventional realistic design and the value of suggestion over reproduction.[8]

Alone with these nascent theories, Craig recalls feeling lost, "I was in a state when I doubted everything – marriage, theatre – friends – career – money matters – all seemed to have cheated me."[9] Craig's healthy penchant for the dramatic over-looks the contributions of two men in particular. In 1893, Craig had befriended brothers-in-law James Pryde and William Nicholson. Artists themselves and ardent theatre fans, the two frequently invited Craig to their home in Buckinghamshire for long conversations on art and theatre. During one such visit, Nicholson even showed Craig the basics of woodblock printing, training Craig would later rely on when creating his groundbreaking theatrical designs.[10]

In the aforementioned *Woodblocks and Some Words*, Craig expounds on both the financial and artistic appeal of woodblock printing. He explains:

> I have produced more wood-engravings than etchings, and more etchings than plays. To wood-engrave and print one's cuts costs so little, say one shilling and nine pence to cut and print one design. To etch and print the plate costs more, say nine shillings or fifteen shillings per design. To pro-duce a play costs a great deal.[11]

After ending his acting career, the only self-earned income source he'd ever known, the low cost of woodblock printing appeared all the more attractive. Indeed, Craig went from designing one woodcut in 1897 to designing 72 in 1898.[12] Coupled with these financial benefits, woodblock printing provided Craig with the artistic freedom he so desired. In his autobiography *Index to the Story of My Days* (1957), Craig recalls, "Sketching, wood-engraving, reading and love-making, I was drifting, searching, and puzzled – but free. Free! No more tied to any one Theatre; I had my Liberty."[13] For years, directors and producers had checked Craig's artistic impulses resulting in uninspired work. Bablet describes one of Craig's early unrealized designs as "show[ing] the direct influence of the Lyceum style in choice and arrangement of scenic elements."[14] With woodblock printing, Craig finally had the artistic space and medium in which to experiment.

Free from the conventional realism of popular theatrical design, Craig by no means experimented in a void. Artistic developments, like the art nouveau poster, greatly inspired the burgeoning artist. Over the past few decades, the manufacturing boom had increased the demand for creative advertisements. First in France and then elsewhere, artists focused their efforts on creating eye-catching posters for products, services, and even theatrical performances. Given the limitations of printmaking, artists moved away from realistic detail opting instead for minimalist strokes and bold swathes of color – many drawing inspiration from Japanese prints.[15] Although slower to adopt the art nouveau poster, by the mid-1890s England welcomed the new art form as evidenced by the 1894 International Artistic Pictorial Poster Exhibition in London. The exhibition showcased the posters of French and English artists including Henri Toulouse-Lautrec, Jules Chéret, and even Nicholson – with whom Craig attended the event.[16]

Analysis of Craig's early work reveals many similarities to the great poster artists of his time. Consider for example Toulouse-Lautrec's "Mademoiselle

Eglantine's Troupe."[17] By 1896, Toulouse-Lautrec – considered by many the "greatest poster designer" of the late 19th century – had already mastered the techniques now associated with art nouveau posters. His colored lithograph, "Mademouiselle Eglantine's Troupe," depicts a chorus line of women, seductively raising their skirts to reveal black stockinged legs. Toulouse-Lautrec's delicate contoured lines deftly suggest the movement of the skirts. While short dashes and curves pattern the closest woman's dress, the figures in the distance become progressively less detailed in a shift towards abstraction.

Despite the disparate mediums and subject matter, Craig's woodblock print "Miss Ellen Terry as Mamillius in "A Winter's Tale"" appears heavily influenced by these techniques.[18] The print depicts Terry in her first role at age eight. Thicker than those of Toulouse-Lautrec, contour lines capture the young girl's boyish figure and haircut. Squiggles decorate her coat, suggesting detail similar to that of the closest woman's dress. Similarly, Terry's left side reflects the same movement towards abstraction. However Craig furthers this abstraction, by creating breaks in the outline. Though the thicker lines could be due to the differing mediums – with lithographs allowing for greater intricacy – the breaks in the outline reveal a conscious move towards suggestion over reproduction. Craig's skilled rendering of Terry's face and collar indicate that he was fully capable of completing the outline but opted not to for stylistic reasons. Even in this simple woodcut Craig experiments with the techniques of his famous contemporaries to develop a style all his own.

Craig's work also riffs on Pryde and Nicholson's woodblock prints. For example, Craig's use of contour lines and small strokes of color in "Miss Terry" closely resembles Pryde's portrait "William Nicholson" published two years prior.[19] However, Craig once again furthers the abstraction through partial outlines. Comparing Nicholson's 1895 bookplate for Phil May to Craig's 1899 portrait of "Miss Terry as "Imogen"" reveals a similar influence.[20] Craig follows Nicholson in using bold, dark hatching, but depicts more of Terry's body and includes scenic elements like a landscape backdrop and curtain masking.

These details anticipate Craig's later assertion that woodblock printing prepared him to design for the stage. "By 1900 I felt I had served a sufficiently long woodcutting apprenticeship to produce a play. You do not see the connection between chopping wood and theatricals, and yet there is one."[21] Craig proceeds to explain this rather abstruse claim by detailing the many ways woodblock prints can aid with theatrical design and publicity. Cutting designs onto wood allowed Craig to print multiple copies of a single design. He could then use those copies to experiment with color and lighting. Woodblock printing proved similarly useful in creating theatrical posters and programs. Craig himself designed the programs for his first three stage productions. In response to the question "Why so much fuss about programs?" Craig retorted, "No other reason than the ordinary wish to have everything in our theatre of the best."[22]

While woodblock printing served Craig well in his later endeavors, it played an even more vital role in the years from 1898 to 1900; having left the theatre, it became a main source of income for Craig. As he explained, "When I left off acting, and threw up eight pounds a week for nothing a month, except what friends would help one to, things looked black..."[23] By the spring of 1898 Craig had left Gibson and moved in with his mistress, Jess Dorynne. Although the two survived off of Dorynne's small allowance, Craig was always in search of supplemental income.

Fortunately, the popularity of arts journals had risen over the past two decades and the demand for submissions along with it. Epitomic of the arts and crafts movement, art journals showcased simple art forms – including woodblock printing – and were frequently crafted by individuals or small printing shops.[24] One such journal warranted an entry in Craig's autobiography:

> Rich inside, 'but the outside to behold' was an astounding sight, and to see it on the little Uxbridge station bookstall of all places was comic. One turned, like a animal rather suspicious of something unexpected – went up to it, and even when one got there, wondered 'What on earth is this *Yellow Book*'...But it was a magazine, although a book, a solid quarterly volume.[25]

The Yellow Book was an illustrated quarterly compiled by John Lane that ran from 1894 to 1897. While *The Yellow Book* may have been the first art journal Craig encountered, it certainly wasn't the last.

Craig began selling his prints piecemeal to various arts journals in 1898 – often capitalizing on his mother's image. In June of that year, Craig had his first success when *The Artist* bought a print of his mother playing Ophelia.[26] Later that year, another print of his mother appeared as a supplemental insert in *The Dome*.[27] The success of the two Terry prints was no coincidence. As Craig colloquially stated, editors demanded "the guv'nor or nothing."[28] Much like the tabloids of today, arts journals published prints of famous figures hoping to draw a following from preexisting fan bases, and Terry had a strong fan base. As the leading lady of the much loved Lyceum Theatre, her many fans desired to know her better - a desire that businesses were quick to capitalize on. From 1897 to 1902, publishers released no fewer than four Terry biographies.[29] Meanwhile businesses secured Terry's endorsements on everything from corsets to soup.[30] Though the amount Craig received for the two Terry prints remains unclear, he later boasted of making 10 shillings for two drawings of Irving.[31] Given Irving's immense popularity, Craig likely earned a slightly lesser amount for the two Terry prints. In other words, piecemeal sales failed to significantly impact Craig's income.

That same year Craig also released the first twelve issues of *The Page*, an artistic journal that he both edited and published. In advertisements, Craig described the journal as, "A monthly magazine containing original prose, poetry, woodcuts, music, bookplates, menus,"[32] although instances of the first two were few and far between. Unlike Craig's later journal *The Mask*, *The Page* consisted predominantly of images. Much of the literature that Craig did include was reprinted from other sources. As Craig justifies in an early issue:

Although the literature in this number has most of it been printed over and over again, still we think we cannot do better than print it once more. The illustrations are however original and are designed and cut in our offices.[33]

Craig's experience editing and printing *The Page* proved invaluable later in his career. According to Olga Taxidou in her analysis of *The Mask*, *The Page* served as a dress rehearsal of sorts in which Craig developed his business sense and artistic style.[34] For example, after a year of monthly issues, Craig shifted *The Page* to a quarterly release. When he released the first issue of *The Mask* almost a decade later, Craig kept the more manageable quarterly format. Likewise, many of Craig's later illustrations show traces of his early experiments with art nouveau.[35] By preparing Craig for the main event, *The Page* provided the platform he would eventually use to develop and disseminate his theatrical ideas. As Taxidou elucidates, "It is in the pages of *The Mask*, possibly more than in any other arena, where Craig's 'Artist of the Theatre' – the director – can take shape and exercise his power unequivocally."[36]

Yet again, Craig appropriated his mother's name and image in order to secure the finances needed to maintain this experiment. In February 1898, not only did Craig include a bookplate of his mother's name, he also drew attention to it in his opening remarks. Craig emphasized that the bookplate was "used by MISS ELLEN TERRY" going on to explain that bookplate collectors could purchase copies by applying to the sub-editor.[37] In June 1898, Craig transformed the aforementioned Ophelia print into a double page supplement. Craig again called the readers' attention to the print in his opening remarks describing it as "a woodcut of Miss Ellen Terry, newly imprinted in its original form, and coloured by hand."[38] None of the other editions include Terry prints but acknowledgements and advertisements show a continued desire to capitalize on his mother's fan base.[39]

Though it provided Craig ample space to experiment artistically, *The Page* was only moderately successful as a financial venture.[40] *The Page* folded in 1901. As Craig lamented, "[*The Page*] cost next to nothing – only my life."[41] The effort of maintaining *The Page*, with little help aside from Dorynne, far exceeded the profits.

In 1899, Craig appropriated his mother's image yet again, publishing *Henry Irving, Ellen Terry, Etc.* Much like *The Page* this booklet eschewed writing in favor of prints and sketches depicting Terry and Irving. Of the 19 plates included in the booklet, eight related to Terry. In addition to the previously published Terry portraits, Craig also included portraits of her as Imogen, Nance Oldfield, Grace Harkaway, and even as an eight-year-old Mamillius. The collection also included the aforementioned sketch of Terry and a print depicting Terry's dressing room at the Lyceum. Herbert Stone of Lakeside Press in Chicago published two editions of the booklet: a standard edition and deluxe edition. Stone printed 400 copies of the standard edition, which sold for $1.50, and only 100 copies of the deluxe edition, which sold for $3.50.[42] To what extent Craig profited from this enterprise remains unclear.

MISS ELLEN TERRY AS OPHELIA, 1898.

E. G. C.

Fig.1. Woodcut on paper of Ellen Terry portraying Ophelia, by her son, Edward Gordon Craig (1872-1966). Ellen Terry played Ophelia opposite the Hamlet of Henry Irving at the Lyceum Theatre in 1878. From the Gabrielle Enthoven Collection, © Victoria and Albert Museum, London.

PORTRAITS: A SON'S CAMPAIGN

Financial necessity drove Craig to exploit his mother's image, yet close analysis of the prints themselves reveals additional motives. Deemphasizing Terry's sexuality, while simultaneously emphasizing her youthful spirit and stubborn strength, Craig attempted to redefine his mother's image. The collection of prints represents the early stages of a campaign for his mother's agency – a campaign Craig would take back up after his mother's death in his biography *Ellen Terry and her Secret Self* (1931).

In 1897, Ellen Terry turned fifty, a dangerous thing for an actress to do. While she remained popular, she became frustrated with the parts she was receiving at the Lyceum. Craig suggested in his biography that at some point in Terry's career people began to question her ability to memorize lines as well as her physical wellbeing. However, Craig adamantly denied that Terry ever "doddered." Instead, Craig reversed the aging process by insisting that Terry refused to memorize unworthy scripts and faked illness to avoid unpleasant tasks.[43]

Craig first attempted this reverse-aging technique with his 1901 portrait "Miss Terry as "Nance Oldfield.""[44] In comparison to photographs of the same production, Craig's print emphasizes Terry's young and playful spirit. The photographs reveal a middle-aged woman, still stunning but with the rounded jaw and heftier build that often accompany aging.[45] Similarly, the photographs portray Terry with wary, submissive expressions - her gaze directed upwards under questioning brows. Craig on the other hand depicts Terry with a much sharper jaw, atop a long, youthful neck. While her gaze is hidden in the shadows, pinpricks of light suggest a peevish rather than submissive attitude. As for her wardrobe, the large expanse of her cloak, artfully suggested with a few contour lines, makes Terry appear smaller. Meanwhile the single-color detail, Terry's red bow, adds a playful air. Insignificant individually, these changes collectively reverse the aging process making Terry appear twenty years younger and fully capable of any role she might deign to portray.

In spite of her aging, Terry remained an object of sexual desire well into middle age. The aforementioned corset endorsement pictures Terry dressed in little more than her undergarments, revealing a large expanse of perfectly white skin. Her lustrous locks flow freely down her back. One hand frames her face while the other arm supports her head as if she is lying down in bed.

Those admirers lucky enough to secure an interview found Terry wonderfully flirtatious. Basing his conclusion on Terry's correspondence with her many admirers, biographer Michael Holroyd goes so far as to claim, "When she was happy it seemed as if Ellen loved everyone."[46] In *The Secret Self*, Craig adamantly negates this claim insisting that Terry never ceased loving his father.[47] Indeed, Craig believed that the two could have reconciled if only Terry hadn't proceeded to marry Charles Wardell Kelly. According to Craig, Terry's romantic dalliances merely helped to pass time and she did not take suitors like George Bernard Shaw "too seriously."[48] To a certain extent, this argument appears to reflect the insecurities of a man who never fully accepted his parents' separation. However, the argument also demonstrates a desire to desexualize his mother's image, transforming her into the subject rather than object of conversation.

Years earlier, in the aforementioned portrait of Terry as Imogen, Craig employed similar tactics. Many photographs of the production captured Imogen the princess. In one, Terry is dressed in extravagant fabrics, draped to emphasize her curves.[49] Together with her elaborate jewelry and crowned head piece, the ensemble clearly eludes to the sensuous "other." With her head tilted back in longing and her fingers drawn to her lips, Terry abandons modern propriety to embody the desirable Imogen.

However, Craig chooses to portray Imogen as a page.[50] After discovering her husband's betrayal, Imogen dresses herself as a boy and sets out on her own. Dressed as a woman Imogen is the object of a man's wrath, but dressed as man she – and by extension Terry – is able to pursue a more promising future. Furthermore, the men's clothing draws the viewer's attention away from her body towards her face. Terry's dark jacket and wrap blend into the gray scenery, while the light on her face reveals a terribly troubled expression worthy of a great actress. Although the white cloud detracts somewhat from this effect, one could imagine an inexperienced or rushed Craig, attempting to direct attention from the cloud to his mother's face.

Perhaps the surest example of Craig's campaign to establish his mother's agency lies not in his portraits of Terry on stage, but in his portrait of Terry in private. In his portrait entitled simply "Miss Terry, Private Portrait," Craig beautifully captures a moment of quiet strength. Terry appears lost in contemplation. Her angular profile, direct stare and downturned lips provide a welcome contrast to the weak, submissive Terry found in photographs. Consider Hollyer's 1886 photograph, for example, one of the only instances where Terry appears in full profile.[51] Rather than staring straight ahead Terry's gaze lifts slightly upward. Together with her down turned brows, the gaze takes on the same submissive quality Terry assumed for many of her roles. Whereas Craig's portrait employs contour lines to suggest a strong jaw, the photograph reveals a softer, rounded jaw line. Likewise the many layers of lace in the photograph appear frivolous in comparison to the classic strand of pearls Terry wears in Craig's portrait.

Although small, these details make for two dramatically different portraits. In Hollyer's photograph, Terry appears weak, subject to the whims of husbands, directors, and producers. In Craig's print however, the audience catches a glimpse of the strong, willful mother Craig described in his later writings. In his biography, Craig asserted, "…I have often known persons who looked on my mother as a rather weak nature. She looked on herself as wretchedly weak – so that settles it for once that she was strong."[52] He later supported this claim with an anecdote, describing a rehearsal in which his mother asked for advice from a director only to completely ignore his notes.

Only by establishing his close connection to his mother could Craig successfully redefine her image. In his biography, Craig dedicates a great deal of writing to establishing this connection. Indeed, he bases the book on the premise that Terry

Fig 2. Ellen Terry with her children Edith and Edward Gordon Craig, 1886, London. Photography by Frederick Hollyer (1837-1933). Used with gratitude to the Victoria and Albert Museum, London.

maintained two distinct personas: the flirtatious, playful actress whom she revealed to all who knew her, and the kind, loving mother whom she revealed only to her closest relatives. Craig explains:

> In every being who lives, there is a second self – sometimes three selves – one of these being very little known to any one. You who read this have a real person hidden under your better-known personality, and hardly anyone knows it – it's the best part of you, the most interesting, the most

curious, the most heroic, and it explains that part of you which puzzles us. It is your secret self.[53]

Craig further warns, "So much lest you go astray when reading of her either in her letters to G.B.S., or the recent Biography of Reade, or in other books about her. Take it quite truly from me that I knew her heart better than anyone else."[54]

With Craig's depiction of his mother's dressing room, he appears to claim a similar level of intimacy.[55] While the room itself is unimpressive – a small closet-like space with a chair and two mirrors – the details provide an intimate view into Terry's life. Craig includes layers of notes pinned to the mirror, multiple coats, framed artwork, photographs, a lamp and even a small table clock. These specific details are unusual both given the challenges associated with woodblock printing and Craig's minimalist style. With each detail, Craig appears to stake a claim, to say, "I know the details of mother's room better than anyone, because I know mother better than anyone."

CONCLUSION: A MOTHER'S IMAGE

After 1900, Craig only dedicated two additional prints to his mother: a costume design for Ibsen's *The Vikings at Helgeland* and a small bouquet framed by Terry's initials imprinted on the cover of *The Secret Self*. In 1901, Terry helped fund Craig's first production venture, Purcell's *Dido and Aeneas* and *The Masque of Love*.[56] Terry also appeared as a curtain raiser, once again allowing her son to profit from her name and image. Although Craig preferred to think of the production as a financial failure – too revolutionary to warrant popular approval – it actually proved quite profitable. As Holland underscores the production actually took in almost double the expenses. Craig also received critical acclaim for his designs, marking the beginning of his career as an innovative theatrical designer and theorist. Craig no longer needed to rely on his mother's image to sell woodcuts.

Nevertheless, the years from 1898 to 1900 marked an important period of experimentation in Craig's life. The relative inexpensiveness of woodblock printing allowed Craig to play with suggestion and abstraction – two qualities which would later come to define his innovative lighting and scenic designs. Editing *The Page* provided invaluable practical experience when he went on to publish his highly influential theories in *The Mask*. Much of this experimentation was funded by appropriating his mother's name and image. By capitalizing on his mother's fame, Craig both supplemented his meager income and championed the strong woman he had relied on all his life. His unique depictions counter images of his mother as sexual object or aging actress, instead highlighting her strength and vitality. Together with *Ellen Terry and Her Secret Self*, these depictions provide a stunning example of a son's campaign for his mother's image – his desire to not only claim a close connection with his famous mother but also to emphasize her own agency in the process.

[1] Edward Gordon Craig, *Woodcuts and Some Words* (London: J.M. Dent & Sons, 1924), 15.

[2] Craig, 99.

[3] Edward Gordon Craig has been praised for his innovative designs and, somewhat controversially, furthering the scope of the director. He eliminated footlights, patented neutral, mobile scenic panels, and called for unified stage pictures. For more information see Dennis Bablet, "Edward Gordan Craig," last modified on January 12, 2019, https://www.britannica.com/biography/Edward-Gordon-Craig.

[4] Peter Holland, introduction to *Index to the Story of My Days*, by Edward Gordon Craig (Cambridge: Cambridge University Press, 1981), ix.

[5] Edward Gordon Craig, *Index to the Story of My Days* (London: Hulton, 1957), 148.

[6] Michael Holroyd, *A Strange Eventful History: The Dramatic Lives of Ellen Terry, Henry Irving, and Their Remarkable Families* (New York: Farrar, Straus and Giroux, 2009), 242.

[7] Edward Gordon Craig, *Ellen Terry and Her Secret Self* (London: Sampson Low, Marston & Company, 1931), 122.

[8] Denis Bablet, *Edward Gordon Craig,* trans. Daphne Woodward (New York: Theatre Arts, 1966), 31.

[9] Craig, *Index,* 197.

[10] Colin Campbell, *The Beggarstaff Posters: The Work of James Pryde and William Nicholson* (London: Barrie & Jenkins, 1990), 14.

[11] Craig, *Woodcuts* xiii.

[12] Craig, *Woodcuts,* 99.

[13] Craig, *Index,* 192.

[14] Bablet, *Edward Gordon Craig,* 18.

[15] Petra Ten-Doesschate Chu, *Nineteenth-century European Art* (New York: Harry N. Abrams, 2003), 471.

[16] Campbell, *The Beggarstaff Posters*, 30.

[17] Henri Toulouse-Lautrec, "Mademouiselle Eglantine'S Troupe, 1896" (New York: Museum of Modern Art).

[18] Edward Gordon Craig, *Henry Irving, Ellen Terry, Etc.* (Chicago: Herbert S. Stone, 1899), n.p.

[19] Craig, *Henry Irving,* n.p.; Campbell, *The Begarstaff Posters*, front cover.

[20] Craig, *Henry Irving,* n.p.; Campbell, *The Beggarstaff Posters,* 44.

[21] Craig, *Woodcuts,* 2.

[22] Craig, 4.

[23] Craig, 15-16.

[24] Olga Taxidou, *The Mask: A Periodical Performance by Edward Gordon Craig.* (Amsterdam: Harwood Academic Publishers, 1998), 3.

[25] Craig, *Index,* 151.

[26] Craig, 200.

[27] Edward Gordon Craig, "Ellen Terry, 1898." *The Dome* 1 (1898): 248.

---

[28] Craig, *Woodcuts,* 16.

[29] The list includes: Walter Calvert, *Sir Henry Irving and Miss Ellen Terry: a Record of Over Twenty Years at the Lyceum Theatre* (London: Henry J. Drane, 1897); Charles Hiatt, *Ellen Terry and her Impersonations: An Appreciation* (London: George Bell and Sons, 1898); Scott Clement, *Ellen Terry* (New York: Fredrick A. Stokes, 1900); Thomas Edgar Pemberton, *Ellen Terry and her Sisters* (London: C. Arthur Pearson, 1902).

[30] For a more complete list, see Katharine Cockin, *Ellen Terry: Spheres of Influence* (London: Pickering & Chatto, 2011), 133-48.

[31] Craig, *Woodcuts,* 16.

[32] Edward Gordon Craig, ed., *The Page* 1 (1898): n. p.

[33] Craig, n.p.

[34] Taxidou, *The Mask,* 7.

[35] Taxidou, 18.

[36] Taxidou, 7.

[37] Craig, *The Page* 1, n.p.

[38] Craig, n.p.

[39] In 1900, Craig dedicated The Christmas Edition of The Page to the "DIVINE OPHELIA OF DRURY LANE," also supplying the date of his mother's performance to prevent any doubt as to the actress in question. When compiling issues of the page into volumes, Craig again relied on his mother's name to sell copies. After a brief description of the 1898 Volume, Craig was quick to recall the Terry print – listing it first among the volume's contents. Likewise, Terry's name appeared first in Craig's description of the 1899 Deluxe Edition. In addition to including cardboard mounted prints, this edition featured twelve original bookmarkers. One boasted the aforementioned Terry bookplate, while another brandished a print of Terry's initials surrounded by a wreath. See Edward Gordon Craig, ed., The Page Christmas (1900): n. p.

[40] As Craig explained, only a few copies were printed and "fewer sold." The first issue sold for one shilling and two pence or seven shillings for twelve months. In 1899, when Craig adopted a quarterly format the subscription price rose to ten shillings a year. As for the scope of the journal, Craig described the original print as "limited." When Craig compiled and reprinted the volumes in later years, he printed anywhere from 12 copies of the 1899 Deluxe Edition to 600 copies of the 1900 Christmas Edition. These were primarily sold in England, with Alfred Bartlett publishing additional copies in America. One advertisement in *The Cornhill Booklet* suggest that Bartlett printed up to 300 copies of the 1900 Volume as well as an unknown quantity of the Christmas Edition and 1901 Volume. For more see, Craig, *Index,* 191; Craig, *The Page* 1, n.p.; Craig, *The Page* Christmas, n.p.; "The Page," *The Cornhill Booklet* 1 (1900): 230.

[41] Craig, *Index,* 191.

[42] "Herbert S. Stone & Company," *The Literary World* 30 (1899):307.

[43] Craig, *Secret Self,* 149.

[44] Craig, *Henry Irving,* n.p.

[45] Window and Grove, "Ellen Terry as Nance Oldfield, 1891," (London: National Portrait Gallery); Window and Grove, "Ellen Terry as Nance Oldfield in "Nance Oldfield," 1891," (London: National Portrait Gallery).

[46] Holroyd, *A Strange and Eventful History,* 178.

[47] Craig, *Secret Self,* 21.

[48] Craig, 97.

[49] Window and Grove, "Ellen Terry as Imogen in "Cymbeline," 1896," (London: National Portrait Gallery).

[50] Craig, *Henry Irving,* n.p.

[51] Frederick Hollyer, "Portrait Photograph of Ellen Terry, 1886," (South Kensington: Victoria and Albert Museum).

[52] Craig, *Secret Self,* 12.

[53] Craig, viii.

[54] Craig, 15.

[55] Craig, *Henry Irving,* n.p.

[56] Holland, introduction, xii-iii.

ON THE CORNER OF 12ᵀᴴ AND CLAIRMOUNT: CONVERSATIONS WITH PLAYWRIGHT DOMINIQUE MORISSEAU, ACTOR BREAYRE TENDER, AND THE GHOSTS OF DETROIT '67

Mary Anderson and Billicia Hines
Wayne State University

On July 23, 2017, Detroit Public Theatre produced a site-specific production of *Detroit '67* by Dominique Morisseau on the hallowed grounds of 12th Street and Clairmount. The most significant work in Morisseau's trilogy of plays The Detroit Project, Detroit '67 is a fictional account of characters whose lives are irreparably transformed during the city's July 1967 uprising. The 1967 Detroit Rebellion, commonly known as the 12th Street Riot, is among the most violent and destructive in the history of the United States. In addition to the loss of forty-three lives and extensive property damage, the events of 1967 and their aftermath have had an abiding impact on the construction of narratives about the city and their relationship to the socio-political realities of those left behind. The corner of 12th and Clairmount were doubly hallowed on this particular summer day in 2017, as we all sat positioned on the precise site where the conflict began, exactly 50 years later.

In what follows, we draw on excerpts from several interviews and conversations with Morisseau and actor Breayre Tender ["Bunny" in the Detroit Public Theatre production], contextualized with critical scholarship as a means to explore and examine the relationship between embodied acts of writing and performing and the politics of place.

Detroit Projects

Dominique Moriseau's trilogy of plays, *Detroit Projects*, have garnered her international attention as a unique voice in the articulation of the black experience. In these three plays, which are all set in the rust-belt city of Detroit, one of the most influential and misaligned cities in the American imaginary,[1] Morisseau explores the form and function of historical representation in dramatic contexts. Each of the plays in the trilogy engages with three of the most significant historical periods for African Americans in Detroit. These three monumental periods of history have had a significant impact in shaping contemporary realities. *Paradise Blue* engages with the vibrant history of the 1940s jazz community in Detroit, emblematic of the renaissance in black arts that was taking place in urban centers across the U.S. at that time. The subsequent displacement of the African American community in Detroit due to processes of gentrification affected this vital arts scene in Detroit as well as undermined the social, economic, and political infrastructure of African Americans. *Paradise Blue* reflects a particular jazz community during the Albert Cobo election: a troubled trumpeter who wants to sell his business; a mysterious woman is on her own. The play examines what tears a community apart, asking "Is it something within or something outside?" *Detroit '67*, the second in the trilogy of plays, deals with the history of the 1967 riots, rebellion or civil unrest that continue to haunt the city - both rhetorically and materially. Morisseau's award-winning *Detroit '67* explores an explosive and decisive moment in a great American city. The play's compelling characters struggle with racial tension and economic instability. *Detroit '67* is a work grounded in historical understanding that also comments meaningfully on the pressing issues of our day. The final work in the trilogy, *Skeleton Crew*, takes on the topic of the auto industry, urban renewal and who it impacts. A makeshift family of workers at the last stamp fix plant in the city discover the plant is closing. The play explores themes of gentrification, "new" vs. "old" Detroit, homelessness, class divisions, violence and the abiding impact of the automotive industry on the mobility and immobility of African Americans in the city.

Morisseau has constructed the narratives in her trilogy in such a way that the history of displacement of African Americans in Detroit is spread out across three points in history, across multiple generations of African-Americans. This distribution of the narrative illustrates the ways in which circumstances of one historical period lead to the next, and contemporary realities can only be understood as a complex and ongoing dialogue between past, present and future. Morisseau's aim in writing these plays was to shed new light on how Detroiters are viewed in the United States. When interviewed by *American Theatre* about her response when Detroiters asked if she was going to make them look good, she said, "I am going to make you look human. Because that's what you are."[2] There is a gravitas embedded within this question and even more embedded within Morisseau's answer, because the question does much more than denote a concern about appearance in the visual sphere. Rather, the question is a reflection of the dehumanization of Detroit residents in the aftermath of 1967, and of the dehumanization of African Americans in the public imaginary for centuries. Morisseau's response to this question and, indeed, Morisseau's scripting of this play, is about a first step toward reconciliation: reconciliation of the conflict that Americans hold about the humanity of black people. As a first step in this process, Morisseau endeavors to restore the humanity of black characters, black bodies on stage. In this respect, her project is intimately intertwined with Genevieve Fabre's argument that black theatre is, "born out of historical conflict ...[in] quest for identity."[3] However, this mission to restore the humanity of black characters, black images, black bodies and black lives is complicated by the illusion that restoration and reconciliation are not necessary. As Ta-Nehisi Coates writes in "The Case for Reparations," "We believe white dominance to be a fact of the inert past, a delinquent debt that can be made to disappear if only we don't look."[4] Morisseau's plays invite audiences to look and to learn, if they are willing. As Morisseau noted in a conversation with article co-author Billicia Hines:

> What I really feel responsible to is humanity. I feel responsible to creating three dimensional characters in everyone, because that's what I owe everybody. I owe everybody some excavating of their humanity. That's what I owe my characters. That's what I owe my people because they have been considered three-fifths of humanity for so long, still now in the Constitution. To me as a writer, if I've made a five-fifths human being out of my own people, then I am already creating a rebellion.[5]

Morisseau's perspective is sensitive to the complex, imaginative and fundamentally politically engaged nature of meaning-making as it transpires in the theatrical encounter. In a Q and A with theatre students at Wayne State University, Morisseau elaborated on the significance of the cycle as it pertains to the political implications of such historical representation:

> **WSU**: As a playwright, but especially as an African American woman, how does it feel for you to know that these plays that you've written about Detroit, are not only informing my generation and generations after me about our history as African Americans in this country, as well specific areas like Detroit? How has that affected you? The response that people have been getting from your work and how much people are learning from your work? How much your work is inspiring young African American artists to write about where they come from or to figure out who they are and where they come from?

> **Dominique Morisseau**: I bring in everything that I'm going through in the moment into every conversation. I just saw *13* yesterday, which is Ava Duvernay's documentary about mass incarceration. ... I love documentaries. They inspire me. They inspire my story telling very much. I saw *Birth of a Nation...* I would not recommend seeing those two things on the same day like I did, unless you have a really high threshold for pain.

I'm saying that because in *Birth of a Nation* ... One was a documentary, one was a movie based on history, but that was a fictional account of history, right? There was a lot of my friends who are all studied and whatever, have some issues with the fictional accounting of *Birth of a Nation*. Not to mention other problems with supporting the film as women, right? For me, I did not have any problems with the fictional accounting of the movie because I don't ever expect something based on history to be a history lesson. I think people often do. I think that's where they get disappointed. They also expect from history to be documentaries, but the Ava Duvernay documentary... I expected that to be accurate with facts and information. I did not expect Birth of a Nation to be that. I expected Birth of a Nation to be a really great story told and inspired by things that happened to Nat Turner, but since Nat Turner's not alive, I didn't expect it to be some kind of accurate depiction of exactly what would have happened. Even if there are documented things about Nat Turner that we knew, that this movie did differently, I just didn't expect it.

I'm saying that I encourage people to go and writers especially, to go into history, if they're interested in history. Maybe they're not. Maybe they're interested in the present. Maybe they're interested in why their mother sang the song she sang in the morning or whatever it is. Whatever interests you, I implore you to go in and investigate the humanity of it. If you're interested in history, I say dig in, but you don't have to become a slave to history. Storytelling and history don't always match. If I told you everything that happened back on a regular day in 1949, it wouldn't shatter you. I'm gonna find an extraordinary day in 1949 to tell the story about. It's gonna be a fictional story, but it's gonna be based on some real stuff. Dizzy Gillespie did come to Black Bottom. Charlie Parker did play. They didn't come to this fake paradise bar/boarding house that I created. That's me.

I think that we can dance with history and know what things we want to maintain the integrity of, but still not betray our imagination, because we gotta have room for our imaginations as writers or what are we doing? Yeah. I'm happy that people look at my work and feel like they're getting to know ... For me, not so much ... Yes, the history, but my intention is not to teach you about the Detroit riots or to teach you about Paradise Blue. It is for you to go teach yourself, right?

Here's a little bit of a nugget from that world, now go find out whether what I said was true or not. Go read for yourself. Go see. Go see and learn some things. I feel responsible to the truth sometimes. To the facts of the world, but only as much as they help my story. What I really feel responsible to is humanity. I feel responsible to creating three dimensional characters in everyone, because that's what I owe everybody. I owe everybody some excavating of their humanity. That's what I owe my characters. That's what I owe my people because they have considered three-fifths of humanity for so long, still now in the Constitution. To me as a writer, if I've made a five-fifths human being out of my own people, then I am already creating a rebellion.

The political dimension of Morisseau's invitation for audiences to engage with her work is made even more clear by a note from the playwright printed in the program for *Detroit '67*:

Playwright's Rules of Engagement

You are allowed to laugh audibly.

You are allowed to have audible moments of reaction and response.

My work requires a few "um hmms" and "uhm hnnns" should you need to use them. Just maybe in moderation. Only when you really need to vocalize.

This can be church for some of us, and testifying is allowed.

This is also live theater and the actors need you to engage with them, not distract them, or thwart their performance.

Please be an audience member that joins with others and allows a bit of breathing room. Exhale together. Laugh together. Say "amen" should you need to.

This is community. Let's go.

peaceandlovedominique :)

Arguably, even if not read, Morisseau's rules are tacitly, implicitly and explicitly understood by the audience in attendance at the 50th anniversary production of *Detroit '67* in a way different from an audience in attendance at Detroit Public Theatre's black box space. The community attending the site-specific performance has a cultural relationship to these "rules" and, further, due to the nature of the memorial context of the performance, the practices of call-and-response and invocation are all the more pertinent. What eventuates is that the attention toward the sonic landscape then welcomes the complexity of the ambient sounds of the environment as much as it invites the "need to speak" from audience members. At one point, a heated conversation transpires a hundred yards across the street from the performance. Voices in conflict pour into the sonic environment due to a situation having nothing to do with the play, itself. Yet this dimension is influential in an ambiguous, elliptical way, which parallels the ricochet of meaning and information as characters within the play describe their experiences of police brutality in a 1960's setting while actual, contemporary police men and women surround the performance to protect the performers and audience members.

Speaking with Hines, Morisseau describes the significance of appreciating and occupying a black cultural perspective as an artist:

> **DM:** You should not be touching my play if you're coming out talking about "We're all one." You're the wrong (person) for this play right now. To me it drives me crazy if there's an artist outside of a culture who just completely negates that there are cultural differences. That to me is not okay. I think often what we see when we have seen a failure of a white director directing a work of color is a failure to recognize our different cultures. You think because you're interested in us that we're the same. Honestly even with black directors. To me I'm more interested in a director that understands that cultural experience in the work, that we have different cultural experiences and that black culture is a culture. It is not white American culture. It is its own particular culture. There is a black culture. There are people that are afraid to admit that black culture exists and I can't rock with any of them no matter what race they are, because then they don't understand my work because my work is absolutely from a black cultural perspective. It does not mean that it's not universal but here's what I mean.

> Me and my husband laugh because I was like, this is what I'm going to use all the time now when I talk about people from outside of a culture working on something and they're not in recognition that a culture exists that they're not a part of. One time we were doing *Skeleton Crew*, we were working on it. This is not to disrespect my dramaturg, he was a lovely guy. This is to give an example of there is a culture that exists that you're not necessarily a part of, even though we're all in America. Black culture means something in a universal play like *Skeleton Crew*. We get to this part in the play where Faye says a line, she has a line. My dramaturg who's outside of my culture, who when somebody was saying "What does it matter? He's a great dramaturg ..." My dramaturg, who's outside of my culture, says to me something's not working in my play. He's not going to control it but he's saying "There's something that's not working right now in that line. We need to fix it because Faye, she's losing her job, she might be losing her pension, she's got this situation with Reggie, and she says to Reggie, when Reggie says 'They could take away your pension.' She says to Reggie 'I wish they would take away my pension.' Why would she wish that?"

> [*laughter*]

> Do you know what I mean? Every time I tell this to a group of black folks they do exactly what you just did.

> **Billicia Hines**: He has no understanding of black folks.

> **DM**: I don't even need to say that. If I'm in a mixed-race room, if I said what I just said right now the whole audience that is of color would start cracking up. Right? Maybe some other folks but definitely the black folks

will start cracking up. If you're not laughing then you don't get something. ... It's fundamental. It's fundamental.

BH: We're always like that, "I wish somebody would do this." That's how we talk. That's how we express ourselves.

DM: Exactly. "I don't know why she would wish they would do that. That line doesn't make sense." I didn't have to say nothing else because my cast started laughing. I just looked at him and they whole cast was like, "No." He got it. We got it. That's what I said, "He got it," because as soon as we laughed he goes "Nevermind. Nevermind." Let's just say for instance my cast wasn't there, and let's just say for instance that I wasn't clear that we were having a bump on culture. I could just go "Why doesn't that line work?" And change my play. Change something that works very well because someone outside of the culture is now dictating a culture they don't understand. That's a problem. ... That's a problem because you're not aware a black culture exists. That means that we have differences in the way that we speak. "It's not that different." "No it's different." Black people say I wish a motherfucker ... There's a whole joke. There's a whole joke that Ced the Entertainer-

BH: Yeah. If someone took my seat. "I wish somebody would take my seat. I wish they would." Then with white people it's like I hope. I hope everything's going to go okay. It's so true. It's so true.

DM: It's true. He made the joke. I can ask a number of people "Have you ever watched Kings of Comedy?" If you haven't watched Kings of Comedy that's going to go over your head "I wish you would". Since he revived that in his joke that's on all of our consciousness for the last 10 years. There's a culture is all I'm trying to say and when you ignore the culture you ignore some very important things about a person's work and about the world they're creating. I can't work with anybody who cannot acknowledge. I don't want anybody directing my play, and I can't control who's doing it in the region all the time, but I can say ultimately I don't want anybody directing my work that doesn't understand that I write from a very particular cultural aesthetic; and that is not willing to learn what that cultural aesthetic is.

Living Ghosts

This cultural-specificity rings loudy in the aesthetic space that is created in the context of *Detroit '67* and, in particular, the site-specific memorial production of the play, inviting a shift from "looking" towards "seeing," as articulated by famed critic John Berger. Berger writes, "seeing... establishes our place in the surrounding world...The relation between what we see and what we know is never settled."[6] Looking allows one to only see things in a mechanical way; seeing takes looking into a deeper level. Breayre Tender, a recently-graduated MFA from the Wayne State Department of Theatre and Dance, delivered what we both felt was the most compelling performance of the 50th anniversary memorial production. This was characteristic of the work that she had done throughout her three years as a graduate student with us. But there was something even more striking about the way that she connected to her character and embodied not only the circumstances of the play, but also somehow seemed to capture the urgency and precariousness of the historical moment that the play represented. We wanted to know how she arrived at this place, what conceptual and somatic tools she used to get there, and what the production meant to her over a year after it was over. We were interested in how her work as an actor in this specific production also invited a shift from "looking" toward "seeing," and so we reached out to her to discuss her embodied memory of creating the role, touching on salient details of the research and process that she undertook to connect with what she describes as "the energy of the time."

Tender began the conversation by telling us a bit about her background growing up in Philadelphia and then in later adolescence in the Central Valley of California. Although she had substantial training in dance and a love of the arts, she was hesitant to pursue arts training at the college level due to family pressures to find a major that would lead to a reliable career after graduation. Nonetheless, inspired by a number of encouraging professors at California State University, Fresno, she ultimately landed in theatre and was recognized with an Irene Ryan Award that led to a scholarship to study the Michael Chekhov technique. As a dancer, the psychophysical approach to training was especially resonant for Tender. Through different psychophysical exercises, actors in the Chekhov technique helps actors develop a sensation of inspiration and learn to trust their own artistic individuality. As a holistic approach, the Chekhov technique emphasizes synergy between the body, imagination, emotions, and intellect. The technique relies on the imagination rather than exclusively on personal history. This process allows the performer to begin from their heart center when they can immediately connect creatively instead of rationally.

Informed by this technical background, Tender began her research on her character, "Bunny," who is Chelle's best friend in *Detroit '67*. A number of lived experiences in the city contributed to her research - including observations about the unique nature of segregation in the Detroit metro area and a visit to the Charles H. Wright Museum of African American History's exhibit *Say It Loud: Art, History, Rebellion*, which documented the history of the 1967 Rebellion in the city. Whereas her childhood experiences in Philadelphia and Stockton were marked by segregation, Tender observed that, nonetheless, people of different backgrounds would "inter-mingle." This she felt was not the case in Detroit, as she experienced in her life in the city over the three years of her MFA studies. It was further amplified once the *Detroit '67* production went on tour and she performed in numerous schools and community centers. Yet, in her research at the *Say It Loud* exhibit, she noticed that documentary photos and videos illustrated that participants in the rebellion were both black and white, destabilizing the narrative that the riots were an exclusively black experience. Attempting to untangle the conflicted accounts of the past and their implications for the present in Detroit, Tender immersed herself in a wide range of artifacts from the time and conducted interviews with people who had lived through and participated in the Rebellion. In this way, she was able to access the "energy" of the people and the time, which she felt was crucial to the development of her role:

> I just felt the energy of everything that has happened here and how it has affected the energy of the people, the psyche of the people ... And I took that energy and I made sure that that was the root of my character - because I knew that anyone that came and saw the shows would immediately be able to connect to or relate to that exact same energy, whether they were around during the time of the riot, whether they have been number that told them about it, that energy that circulated during that time, the same energy that comes out of people that tell the stories about that time.

> And then after that I then went deeper into talking to people around Detroit that were much older than me, that did live during the time of the riots. And just hearing their stories and watching their mannerisms when they re-told these stories ... I made sure that I paid great attention to the details of that [storytelling] because that was again the energy of the time.

Tender's account of her experience developing the role of "Bunny" calls to mind Suzan-Lori Parks' *Elements of Style*, and in particular the section entitled "ghost:"

> *ghost*

> A person from, say, PastLand, from somewhere back there, say, walks into my house. She or he is always alone and will almost always take up residence in a corner. Why they're alone I don't know. Perhaps they're coming missionary style - there are always more to follow. Why they choose a corner to stand in I don't know either - maybe because it's the intersection of 2 directions - maybe because it's safe. They are not *characters*. To call them so could be an injustice. They are *figures, figments, ghosts, roles, lovers* maybe, *speakers* maybe, *shadows, slips, players* maybe, maybe *someone else's pulse.*[7]

Tender's central focus on energy and atmosphere in the development of her performance exceeds some of the typical parameters associated with "character," conventionally defined. Because Tender felt a particular obligation to understand and inhabit the *actual* past - interacting with artifacts and testaments to that actual past in the development of her work - she was directed towards the paradigms of "energy" and "atmosphere," which more closely align with the dimensions of personhood outlined by Parks, and which call upon the energies—or "ghosts"—of 12th and Clairmount, making space integral for this site-specific production .

Morisseau is writing these moments in time from a 21st-century perspective. As a playwright of what Mikell Pinkney calls, "The New Age Post-Revolutionary Era," *Detroit '67*'s purpose is "to look at the past with learned perspectives of the present, leading the way into new, different, and better future."[8] For the past fifty years, the memory of the Detroit Rebellion has been experienced as an unresolved blemish, a scar on the city with profoundly deep, devastating and far-reaching impacts. The memory of the Detroit Rebellion has been governed and produced largely by polarized, bifurcated notions about race, class and history, itself. Attending to the fundamentally aporetic space achieved through the temporal frictions and inconsistencies we find in art enables new space for reflection on these circumstances and, one would hope, forms of reconciliation based on the fundamental principles of unknowing. It is in this spirit that John Baldacchino recommends that we embrace art's "groundless forms of meaning" which are "beyond product and process."[9] In order to do this, however, one must contemplate the ways in which art is neither product nor process:

> Art is not a product, even when there seems to be an object called art. Likewise art cannot be reduced to a process, even when many make an argument for art as a process in order to avoid it becoming a product. To define art from within the paradoxical assumption that it is an in-between would help us understand the art form's open character.[10]

Ultimately, then, it is not only that Morisseau has created a structural or dramaturgical intervention by creating a trilogy of plays that disrupts our perceptions and expectations of history. She has, further, invited performers to participate in a complex choreographed dance between the past and present, between fiction and non-fiction in which the affective space of shame can be unearthed, encountered, and mined as a form of restorative justice.

---

[1] Arjun Appadurai, *Modernity at Large: Cultural Dimensions of Globalization* (Minneapolis: University of Minnesota Press, 1996).

[2] Evans, Suzy. "Dominique Morisseau Is Telling the Story of Her People." AMERICAN THEATRE. January 05, 2017.

[3] Geneviève Fabre, *Drumbeats, Masks, and Metaphor: Contemporary Afro-American Theatre* (Cambridge, MA: Harvard University Press, 1983), 1.

[4] Ta-Nehisi Coates, "The Case for Reparations," *The Atlantic* (August 17, 2017).

[5] Morisseau, Dominique. "Chat with Dominique." Online interview by author. October 10, 2016

[6] John Berger, *Ways of Seeing: Based on the BBC Television Series with John Berger,* (London: British Broadcasting, 2012), 5.

[7] Suzan-Lori Parks, "Elements of Style," The America Play and Other Works (New York: Theatre Communications Group, 1995), 16-17.

[8] Mikell Pinkney, "The Development of African American Dramatic Theory: W.E.B. DuBois to August Wilson- Hand to Hand!" *August Wilson and Black Aesthetics*, eds. Sandra Garrett Shannon and Dana A. Williams, (New York, NY: Palgrave Macmillan, 2011), 30.

[9] John Baldacchino, "The Praxis of Art's Deschooled Practice,"JADE 27.3 (2008), 241-260.

[10] Ibid., 244.

TEXAS EDUCATIONAL THEATRE ASSOCIATION
SCHOLARS DEBUT PAPERS PROJECT

Texas Theatre Journal remains proud of and committed to our involvement with the Texas Education Theatre Association's *Scholars Debut Papers Project*.

Each year, we publish the winning papers from students throughout Texas, showcasing the excellent scholarship and teaching occurring daily throughout our state. This very often marks the very first scholarly publication on students' vitae and helps to encourage them toward further adventures in theatre scholarship.

This volume's award-winners are:

Amanda Rose Villarreal, University of Colorado Boulder,
"It Happens Here: Enacting Change Through Theatre Education"
(featured on page 1 of this volume)

Margaret E. Boos, Texas A&M Commerce,
"A Woman's Place: Lisa Loomer and Gender Inequalities in Parenting Expectations"
(featured on page 75)

Bruce Turk, Texas State University,
"Flips, Quips, and Broken Bits: The Shards of Comedy in Beckett's *Endgame*"
(featured on page 85)

Details about TETA's Scholars Debut Papers Project, including information for students and instructors on how to submit work for award-consideration, may be found on page 120.

A WOMAN'S PLACE: LISA LOOMER AND GENDER INEQUALITIES IN PARENTING EXPECTATIONS

Margaret E. Boos
Texas A&M University Commerce

Gender parity has become a goal for many theatres, however—as evidenced by the data—this goal remains far from actualized. Rob Weinert-Kent reports in 2017 when analyzing plays produced by TCG member theatres, 62% of scripts produced were written by men and only 26% written by women.[1] This data speaks to the marginalization of female playwrights on American stages across the nation. This disparity of representation on the stages of American theatres limits the contribution of women's voices to the national dialogue, and the stories our stages tell. By celebrating women, their work, and their stories, American theatres could initiate conversations to help dismantle patriarchal systems of oppression such as unequal gender parenting responsibilities in heterosexual couples. Lisa Loomer through three of her plays, *Expecting Isabell*, *Living Out*, and *Distracted* exposes the gender inequalities in parenting expectations which favor the male parent and reveals the emotional and physical toll levied on women.

Lisa Loomer currently has her work produced throughout the country, and as a female playwright, provides insight into many issues facing women today. *The Waiting Room* [1994] catapulted Loomer to the national scene and remains her most popular work.[2] She also gained recognition for co-writing the screenplay for *Girl Interrupted.* In educational theatre, her works *Distracted* and *¡Bocón!* remain frequently produced. Additionally, Loomer wrote a commissioned piece for the 2016 Oregon Shakespeare Festival entitled *Roe* chronicling the relationship between Norma McCorvey and Sarah Weddington, the plaintiff and lawyer of the Roe v. Wade Supreme court case respectively.[3] Washington D.C.'s Arena Stage also produced the piece in January 2017 during the famed Women's March. Many

[Women's March] protestors attended the show, and the audience responded to the work enthusiastically.

> By the play's second act, the atmosphere in the theatre had taken on some of the charge of the previous day's rally, and the cast was pausing frequently to accommodate applause. The audience sprang to its feet after the last line, spoken in unison by Weddington and McCorvey: "As of this moment, with the Supreme Court behind us, Roe still stands."[4]

Loomer's *Roe* earned her the 2017 Literary Award for Drama from PEN Center USA.[5]

Loomer's plays defy categorization. Peterson and Bennett write "Lisa Loomer's plays are an exciting mélange of styles and forms: she depicts serious topics with bold dashes of humor."[6] Her plays not only employ a variety of stylistic choices, but thematically they range from women's medical issues, motherhood, attention deficit disorder, Latinx issues, immigration, and abortion rights. "Despite the veneer of zany humor, Loomer fearlessly dives into timely issues: body image, breast cancer, and alternative medicine."[7] Many of her plays center on issues pertaining to women, however she defies any specific labels and address a variety of topics, often within single works.

While Loomer's works thematically cover a range of issues, three of her major works address different aspects of the experience of motherhood. *Expecting Isabel*, *Living Out*, and *Distracted* directly address the complicated experience of becoming a mother and mothering. *Expecting Isabel* follows a couple's journey through infertility and adoption, or the process of becoming a mother. *Living Out* explores the struggles between mothering and working. *Distracted* address the experiences of mothers whose children have a-typical behavior challenges. Through these works, Loomer offers a distinct shift from much of the cannon of American dramatic literature. Arthur Miller's *Death of a Salesman* and *All My Sons* portray mothers as the long-suffering, loyal wife whose life revolves around husband and children. Tennessee Williams in *Glass Menagerie* shows an over-bearing, neurotic mother, but whose entire existence still revolves around her children. Lorraine Hansberry's *A Raisin in the Sun* offers two portrayals of motherhood, but neither woman is afforded an identity outside of their relationship to Walter, the leading male. While the female characters may voice displeasure with situations and circumstances, the texts fail to deliberately examine the unequal burden of parenthood placed on women as opposed to the male parent.

The reflections of motherhood with the dramatic literature cannon directly reflect the social constructs of motherhood in American culture. Parenting magazines,

Pinterest, and social media reinforce the pressure for women to perform unrealistic expectations of motherhood. Mothers are given tips to throw magazine worthy birthday parties with themed snacks and handmade décor. Advice to mothers include encouragement to breastfeed and touts the medical benefits with little honesty about the pain and difficulty or advice to achieve breastfeeding goals. Mothers unable to breastfeed, or those who choose different options for themselves, often face severe social backlash. Pregnant women and new mothers receive unsolicited advice and birthing stories, and strangers feel entitled to touch bellies and ask intensely personal questions about women's cervixes, breasts, vaginas, uteruses, and other areas of the body otherwise considered too personal for questions. Sofia Jawed-Wessel in her TED talk explains how this ultimately objectifies expecting mothers. "When a woman becomes pregnant, she leaves the realm of men's sexual desire and slides into her reproductive and child-rearing role. In doing so, she also becomes the property of the community, considered very important but only because she's pregnant."[8] Social structures completely dehumanize women when they choose to embark on the journey of motherhood by turning them into objects whose sole existence is to create and nurture children.

Research suggests most women experience conflicting emotions as they embark on the journey of motherhood. Society, however, often depicts motherhood as a euphoric experience, with mothers who experience any other emotions as deviant or mentally ill. The societal expectation often leaves mothers feeling even more shame over their conflicting emotions. P. Choi, C. Henshaw, S. Baker and J. Tree documented the feelings in new mothers as they adjusted their self-identity to include motherhood. "For the vast majority of the women, motherhood had either not been what they expected, or they had not known what to expect."[9] The study found women's pre-motherhood expectations as informed by the cultural ideology of motherhood differed from reality. Furthermore, the study suggested these feelings contributed to greater depression and feelings of guilt in mothers as they adjusted to the reality of motherhood while feeling as though they failed to meet social expectations. Women reported resenting crying infants or being unable to care for the baby due to physical limitations after childbirth. These feelings left women feeling guilty and as though they had failed as mothers.[10] The pressures on women as they parent stem from unrealistic societal expectations, thus showing the rarity of honest representations of the realities of motherhood.

Numerous studies document the cultural expectations for women engaging in motherhood, and the inequalities between the expectations for women and men in their parenting duties. Lyn Craig and Killian Mullan found in a multi-nation study "mothers did a significantly higher proportion of total household care than did fathers on all measures. This held true across all household types and across all countries."[11] Additionally, Craig and Lyn, and Julie M. Koivunen, *et al* found the gender inequalities remained consistent despite the mother's professional commitments. "Increasing levels of maternal employment over the past five decades have not resulted in more equitable gender distribution of housework and childcare time."[12] Furthermore, despite attempts at "egalitarian relationships. . . heterosexual couples often fall into more traditional gender roles after they become parents."[13] The gender inequalities not only included amount of work. Fathers contributed to more non-routine care while mothers performed most routine care and care performed solo.[14] Despite great strides in equality for women, patriarchal notions of domestic duties continue to dominate household structures.

Sharon L. Green addresses representations of motherhood in two of Loomer's works, *Living Out* and *Distracted*, in the article *What Does it Take to Be a "Good Mother."* Green's feminist analysis explores the gender inequity with parenting expectations as portrayed in Loomer's work. In exploring *Living Out* and *Distracted*, Green argues the two works present antithetical viewpoints. "The former provides fertile ground for productive moments of exhilaration for feminist spectators, but the latter reinforces patriarchal notions of what constitutes 'good mothering'."[15] Green argues the representations of motherhood in Loomer's work continue to perpetuate the gender inequality in parenting expectations. However, Loomer's work exposes the gender inequities and thus provides opportunities for greater social awareness of the burden on women who become mothers. Exposing "patriarchal notions" of parenting and laying bare the pressures and stress experienced by women actually works to dismantle the inequalities by revealing their inherent hypocrisies.

Loomer's *Expecting Isabel* addresses the beginning of the journey into parenthood. *Expecting Isabel* shows a heterosexual couple's struggles with infertility and adoption, mostly told from the woman's point of view. An under-studied play, *Expecting Isabel* reveals the burden of conception placed on women and explores the challenges and judgements faced by couples who struggle to conceive. Ten lines into the play, Miranda's husband Nick shares he'd love to have a child. While Miranda expresses trepidation stemming from fears of her parents' mental health issues and the quality of the school system, she agrees to try. After being unable to conceive within several months, Miranda buys a book with tips to increase their chances to conceive. Immediately, Loomer reveals the gender disparity in expectations of child conception and family planning. While Nick had initially broached the desire for a child, and Miranda voiced hesitation, the burden of research and problem-solving still falls to the women. Additionally, when Miranda reports the tips from the book to Nick, Nick greets the advice with little enthusiasm.[16] Through this display of the gender inequality in ensuring conception, Loomer reveals how early women bear the burden of parenthood. While Nick urged Miranda to try for a baby, he assumes Miranda will do the actual work of making that happen.

Loomer purposefully crafts dichotomous experiences for the female versus the male to display the burden women face, and the expectation for them to do the emotional work of managing conception. After Nick agrees to see a doctor with Miranda, the doctor places Miranda on serious medication with a litany of side effects. Additionally, they undergo expensive IVF treatments requiring semen samples to be delivered within an hour and a half. However, Miranda, not Nick, must ensure the proper collection of the sample and the delivery.

> MIRANDA. And on the day of my insemination, I woke up at six with a migraine and set about getting a sperm sample from my husband who, not being a morning person, wanted me to dress up a little to help him out. So I put on a bustier and some black stockings over my bloated body.[17]

The juxtaposition of the obstacles faced by Miranda and Nick highlight the gender inequalities. Miranda suffers from a migraine, an extremely painful headache often accompanied by other issues such as nausea. She also experiences swelling, a side effect of the hormonal medication. Nick simply has an aversion to morning. Despite Miranda's extra burdens, she must dress up to entice her husband and ensure the collection of the sample. Loomer's work lays bare the cultural expectation for women to ensure the creation of babies, despite the need for equal female and male DNA to create the embryo.

Loomer sharpens the focus on the inequality of patriarchal notions of parenthood by making the fertility issue rest squarely on the man's shoulders: slow moving sperm. This situation also provides exploration of the gender bias in Western medicine concerning fertility issues. Despite issue stemming from the faulty male haploid cells, the expectation remains for Miranda, the female partner, to seek out the specialists, take the drugs, receive hormone injections, and deliver samples. The doctor never offers hormone therapy or medicine for Nick's sperm; Miranda's body is expected to compensate for his. Loomer's work displays the gender inequalities present at the earliest stages of parenthood and reveals that Western medicine has failed women as well by placing the burden of fertility squarely on female shoulders.

Exploring the next stage of parenting, Loomer's work *Living Out* portrays the relationship between two working mothers: one white, upper-middle class lawyer and the other a Latina woman hired as a nanny. While much has been written about this work, most of the focus has centered on the racial disparity in the play. While certainly an important theme, Loomer also includes many scenes between the husbands and wives revealing truths about the unequal burden of childcare responsibilities on the female partner, and the intersection of such expectations across racial divides. Green argues "The action of *Living Out* does contradictory cultural work by revealing the class assumptions implicit in the ideology of intensive mothering yet simultaneously re-inscribing the traditional gender roles on which it is based."[18] However, as Green notes with the racial ideologies, the act of revealing the cultural gender norms and their negative effects on women actually begins the work of dismantling the oppressive structures. While Loomer does portray women subjected to traditional patriarchal notions of parenthood, these scenes reveal the toll on women, and serve to expose the inequity as opposed to furthering the gender stereotypes.

Throughout *Living Out,* scenes between the husband and wives reveal the gender disparity in parenting expectations. Loomer begins in Scene Two with dialogue between Ana, the woman hired as a nanny, and her husband Bobby overlapping with Nancy, the mother returning to work, and her husband Richard. Conflict begins early when Ana reveals Bobby may need to get their son after school.

> ANA. *(carefully)* Pues . . . Maybe I'm going to need you to pick him up sometimes—
>
> BOBBY. Oh si? So you could take care of somebody else's kid instead of your own son?[19]

Green categorizes this exchange as supporting the patriarchal ideologies of parenthood.[20] However, Loomer explicitly reveals the stress and burden this places on Ana. Additionally, the choice of language when Bobby says "your own son" as opposed to "our son" reveals his assumption that Ana should manage most of the duties of raising and caring for a child. While Ana's work will be more stable than Bobby's construction job, the inconvenience of Ana's employment becomes a source of contention for her husband. It never occurs to him that he has an equal responsibility to pick up their son.

A similar exchange occurs immediately after with Nancy and Richard. However, this exchange also reveals Nancy's personal satisfaction in working and the intrinsic role that plays in her self-identity. As Nancy discusses her trepidations about hiring someone else to care for their child, Richard tries to suggest that Nancy stay home instead of returning to work. She quickly rebuffs him,

> NANCY. *(Lightly)* Well, I have to go back to work, don't I?
>
> RICHARD. Well, how do you define "have to"?
>
> NANCY. *(Laughs)* If I don't go back I'll get fired?
>
> RICHARD. They can't fire you, you're an attorney, you'll sue.

NANCY. Then I'll be on "The Mommy Track." I won't have a prayer in hell of making partner – *(laughs)* And then what have the last sixteen years of my life been for? ... We talked about all of this when I got pregnant –

RICHARD. I know. I just thought we could take this time right *now* to enjoy –

NANCY. Besides, we're going to need my salary with the new mortgage, honey.[21]

The exchange continues with Nancy affirming she always intended to return to work, and they need the money. Nancy's job pays more than Richard's. However, despite Richard using the first-person plural pronoun "we" when talking about taking time, Loomer makes clear he doesn't me "we," but "she." She, the mother, should stay home. Richard never suggests giving up his job, despite Nancy earning more. Furthermore, unlike Ana who only works out of economic necessity, Nancy expresses a desire for professional achievement. Her work is important to her self-identity. However, Richard suggests she simply give it up for the child they both created. As with Ana and Bobby, Loomer subtly reveals the stark, unequal gender expectations in parenting. Neither man can conceive of an option where he might assume the role of primary care-giver while their wife acts as the breadwinner. However, the juxtaposition of the two couples, and the clear focus on the woman's need to work, shows Loomer expects the audience to examine the hypocrisies of these traditional gendered expectations of parenting roles.

In *Distracted*, Loomer explores the journey of a mother searching for answers about her son's behavior issues. Despite much of the marketing and critical reviews focusing on the diagnosis of A.D.D., the work explores the burden, cost, and stress of motherhood. Told through the character only named Mama, we experience her journey in seeking answers and help. Loomer, more than any other work before, shows in *Distracted* how becoming a mother can completely dismantle a woman's identity leaving her named only Mama. While similarly named Dad comes in and out of the conflict, he is belligerent about the entire proceedings, and even refuses to participate in the dramatizations at times. While Dad does help make meals and take care of bedtime duties, he expresses annoyance at having to attend parent-teacher conference, doctors' appointments, and refuses to participate in behavior modification therapies.

DR. ZAVALA. So! How's it going?

MAMA. Well, my husband said it wasn't fair for Jesse to earn points to ride his bike, because exercise is necessary for a child. He also said Jesse should get some warnings before losing points – *(Dad comes on)*

> DAD. He also said he knew an excellent place to *put* the poker chips! *(He gives a thumb's up and leaves)*
>
> DR. ZAVALA. *(annoyed)* Well, it is essential that both parents be on the same page –.[22]

Mama frequently asks for Dad to share in the exploration of solutions for the behavior issues, but he chooses to opt of the actual labor of solving the issues while continuing to exert control over medical decisions and responses to behavior concerns. Green argues this continues to "normalizes gender roles that support contemporary motherhood ideology."[23] Later, however, Green notes "This dynamic—Mama making appointments with therapists, teachers, doctors, and a homeopath, and Dad either missing them or leaving early because he needs to work – persists throughout the play. In both plays women are seen struggling to balance work and parenting, men just head to work."[24] Much like Nancy in *Living Out*, Mama expresses desire to have a professional career, yet feels compelled to forgo those desires because of the labor demands of parenthood.

> MAMA. Since I've just quit my job as an interior designer to work at home and focus on my child, I wonder if I should just sneak in a little work for my one freelance client – *(She get the phone and a notebook marked "Jesse")* But decide to call that doctor about Jesse instead.[25]

By staging the disparate burdens on female and male parents, and their inherent inequalities, Loomer's work actually upends the traditional notions of parenting roles and asks the audience to consider why mothers must sacrifice their careers.

Miranda in *Expecting Isabel,* Ana and Nancy in *Living Out*, and Mama in *Distracted* fight for their desire to work and have an identity outside of motherhood. They fight with their husbands in attempts to more equally divide the responsibilities of parenting. Finally, they fight their own feelings of inadequacy and guilt. These characters and their struggles reveal the strain on women as they balance personal desires, marriages, friendships, and parenthood. By upending the traditional conventions of female parents' identities entirely focused on children and devoid of any other interests, Loomer reveals the false narrative surrounding motherhood and the ramifications for women. Additionally, Loomer exposes the gender imbalance in parenting expectations, providing an open door for cultural conversations surrounding the expectations of mothers and fathers. The works serve not to maintain patriarchal notions of parenthood, but to dismantle such social structures by revealing their inherent inequalities and the emotional and physical toll levied on women.

[1] Weinert-Kent, Rob. "The Gender & Period Count: The More Things Change…" *American Theatre*, 26 September 2017. Theatre Communications Group, www.americantheatre.org/2017/09/26/the-gender-period-count-the-more-things-change/.

[2] Patterson, Jane T. and Susanna Bennet. *Women Playwrights of Diversity: A Bio-bibliographical Sourcebook.* Westport: Greenwood Press, 1997.

[3] Taylor, Kate. "A Playwright Finds Drama, and Humor, in Roe v. Wade." *The New York Times*, 24 Aug 2016. NYTimes.com, www.nytimes.com/2016/08/28/theater/lisa-loomer-abortion-play-roe.html.

[4] Caplan-Bricker, Nora. "A Play About Roe v. Wade That Is a Parable of an Exclusionary Women's Movement." *The New Yorker*, 26 Jan 2017.

[5] "Lisa Loomer Wins 2017 PEN Center USA Literary Award for Drama." *American Theatre,* 27 Sept 2017. Theatre Communications Group, www.americantheatre.org/2017/09/27/lisa-loomer-wins-2017-pen-center-usa-literary-award-for-drama/.

[6] Patterson, 217.

[7] Ibid., 218.

[8] Jawed-Wessel, Sofia. "The Lies We Tell Pregnant Women." *TEDx Omaha*, October 2016. TED, www.ted.com/talks/sofia_jawed_wessel_the_lies_we_tell_pregnant_women.

[9] Choi, P., et al. "Supermum, Superwife, Supereverything: Performing Femininity in the Transition to Motherhood." *Journal of Reproductive & Infant Psychology*, vol. 23, no. 2, May 2005, 172.

[10] Ibid.

[11] Craig, Lyn and Killian Mullan. "How Mothers and Fathers Share Childcare: A Cross-National Time-Use Comparison." *American Sociological Review*, vol. 76, no. 6, 1 Dec. 2011, 852-853.

[12] Ibid., 853.

[13] Koivunen, Julie M., et al. "Gender Dynamics and Role Adjustment during the Transition to Parenthood: Current Perspectives." Family Journal, vol. 17, no. 4, Oct. 2009, 323.

[14] Craig, 852.

[15] Green, Sharon L. "What Does it Take to Be a "Good Mother?": Contemporary Motherhood Ideology and the Feminist Potential of Lisa Loomer's Dramaturgy." *Journal of Dramatic Theory and Criticism*, vol. 28 no. 1, 2013, 5.

[16] Loomer, Lisa. *Expecting Isabel*. Dramatists Play Service, 2005, New York, 12-13.

[17] Ibid., 20.

[18] Green, 8.

[19] Loomer, Lisa. *Living Out*. Dramatists Play Service, 2005, New York, 12.

[20] Green, 9.

[21] Loomer, *Living Out*, 13-14.

[22] Loomer, Lisa. *Distracted*. Dramatists Play Service, 2009, New York, 42-43.

[23] Green, 11.

[24] Ibid., 12.

[25] Loomer, *Distracted*, 15.

FLIPS, QUIPS, AND BROKEN BITS: THE SHARDS OF COMEDY IN BECKETT'S *ENDGAME*

Bruce Turk
Texas State University

This essay aims to illuminate the humor embedded in the poetic structure of *Endgame* in order to help actors and directors bring Beckett's page to life on the stage. *Endgame* presents major challenges for actors—particularly for those groomed by American derivatives of the Stanislavsky method. Given circumstances, sensory/response, emotional recall, and other psychological approaches to preparing a role can lead interpreters down an extremely dark road when wrestling with the bleak world painted by this playwright. Counterintuitively, the acting must be rooted in a strong tradition of clowning. The work draws upon the rhythmic verbal patter of British music hall entertainments as well as the physicality of French farce—a physicality that has evolved from the Italian *Commedia dell'Arte* through the interventions of Molière, Labiche, and Feydeau. Analysis of structure reveals the broken comic rhythms of the piece and helps practitioners identify and establish a distance to the given circumstances of the play. Beckett asks for this distance by way of the many self-conscious theatrical references throughout. The characters are certainly aware of them, so the performers should be too. This attitude is as practical as it is theoretical, since the characters themselves establish this distance in an effort to survive in the brutal landscape. "Most interpretations of *Endgame*, in the theatre as well as in criticism, have given up on comedy and gone for tragedy instead. The result has been a production history far more checkered than anything awaiting *Godot*."[1] Without attention to the comedic verbal rhythms, strong physicality, and a self-referential attitude, the characters, the performances, and the production are doomed.

The inner framework of *Endgame* is composed of a wide variety of comic structures. The world of the play is grim and the situation of the characters is dire; yet, the text of the play is carefully built upon a scaffold of comedy. It is "a tragedy that vacillates between terror and farce."[2] It is peopled by clowns (Hamm is a descendant of Pantelone and Clov traces his roots to Arlecchino) and the language is full of comic constructions such as set-ups, punchlines, one-liners, running jokes, story jokes, and physical routines. These amusements may fizzle out or fall flat, but they are comedic nonetheless. These broken bits form the skeleton of the play and contribute to its "macabre mirth."[3] Many of these forms are derived from vaudeville; some date back centuries to the *Commedia dell'Arte*. Close analysis of the *Endgame* text, evidence of Beckett's rehearsal practices, comparisons with other comedic forms, and examples from performance history all demonstrate how the language of the play is not "meaningless patter" as suggested by Esslin,[4] but rather a carefully constructed work containing bits and pieces of identifiable comic repartee.

In his landmark work, *The Theatre of the Absurd*, Martin Esslin presented a comprehensive view of the work of playwrights such as Beckett, Eugene Ionesco, Jean Genet, and others. He collected a wide variety of their plays together, made general pronouncements about their common characteristics, and shaped an attitude toward them, labeling them "absurdist." Without question, Esslin's work is important. He brought attention to the work of these poets of the theatre and advanced the understanding of Absurdist theatre in a general sense. However, he may have done disservice to some of the plays themselves. Ionesco insisted that a play should be weighed and judged upon its own merits.[5] In other words, one should be careful about what one says of Beckett when speaking of Ionesco. As a case in point, consider Esslin's conviction that "if a good play relies on witty repartee and pointed dialogue, these [absurdist plays] often consist of incoherent babblings."[6]

Contrary to Esslin's statement, *Endgame* proves rich in all kinds of clear, pointed, poetic language. It's packed with delicious comic banter and wit. It's filled with carefully crafted poetic expressions that make use of metaphor, antithesis, alliteration, symbolism, imagery, punning, and wordplay. Nagg's joke about the tailor, for example, is a devilishly funny extended "story joke" constructed of a series of intricate smaller jokes, each peppered with puns and scatological wordplay: "A smart fly is a stiff proposition."[7] This evocative language leads us directly into the personality of the characters. Inadequate as it may seem for both Beckett and his characters, language is character and the route to playing these roles passes directly through their text. Of course, this isn't to say that the work is not physical— performing these characters requires astute corporeal skills—but without a crisp attention to the farcical nature of the text, the playing falls flat. The actor must wring meaning from every word. Expressing the inexpressible predicament of the human condition involves a struggle, and this action—this desperate struggle to encapsulate and communicate one's experience—informs the approach to every character in the play.

Endgame presents the bleak spectacle of a man clinging to life as he faces the darkness of death. Hamm is the king of a dying world, peopled only by his parents Nagg and Nell (nightcapped, legless and relegated to a pair of old ash bins) and his personal servant, Clov, who is cursed by the fact that he cannot sit down. The action takes place in the "bare interior" of a room enclosed by "hollow brick" walls.[8] Two small, curtained windows stand high enough that one can only look through them with the aid of a step ladder. It is a stark, barren world where "there's no more nature."[9] Life can no longer take hold in the arid landscape. Seeds are planted, but it doesn't rain and "the whole place stinks of corpses."[10] The sun, apparently, has disappeared and all is "gray...gray...GRAY."[11] The seashore can be seen, but there is no more tide. 100-kilometer winds tear up the dead pine trees. The disintegration evident in the landscape mirrors Hamm's own degeneration; yet, in spite of these dismal circumstances, he willfully clings to life with a macabre, sarcastic appreciation of the situation. "Can there be misery—loftier than mine?"[12] When the appearance of a flea brings hope of procreation and the continuance of life, Hamm ironically points out, "Humanity might start from there all over again."[13] He admonishes Clov for whining about their state: "Use your head, can't you, you're on earth, there's no cure for that!"[14] For all its sense of the vagaries and monotonies of life, the play is rife with this rich sense of what Harold Clurman called Beckett's "special humor."[15]

Endgame is a play where "metaphysics suddenly takes on a farcical tone."[16] For instance, both Nell and Clov draw allusions to theatrical comedy when they ask "Why this *farce* day after day?"[17] [emphasis mine]. There are scores of theatrical references that add humor to the bleak situation of mankind's final moments: Hamm's, "I'm warming up for my last soliloquy"[18] and Clov's, "This is what we call making an exit," for example.[19] Berlin noted that "this, Clov's only self-reflexive line, cause[s] audience laughter, as it was meant to do."[20] Beckett said that *Endgame* was the play he disliked the least, citing its ability to "claw."[21] Yet, even Joseph Chaikin (who directed a critically well-received production in 1977) conceded that his production had too much of the "cry in it."[22] Clearly, he learned that the bitter pill of the play goes down much better with some sugar.

Cohn points out that entire dialogues in *Endgame* are "built comically" around just a very few words.[23] Kenneth Tynan summed it up well: "One gorges on Joyce and slims on Beckett."[24] Beckett elaborated on this sentiment: "James Joyce was a synthesizer, trying to bring in as much as he could. I am an analyzer, trying to leave out as much as I can."[25] Consider this exchange between Hamm and his servant, Clov:

> HAMM: Why do you stay with me?
>
> CLOV: Why do you keep me?
>
> HAMM: There's no one else.
>
> CLOV: There's no where else.
>
> HAMM: You're leaving all the same.[26]

The characters turn and spin just a few simple words, bandying them back and forth like a ball in a game of tennis. These characters pay acute attention to the simple details of language. They make concerted efforts to shape their experience—their reactions to the world and their places in it—through limited, precise, and conscientious word choice. In rehearsal, actors need to search for, find, then savor these precious words. In the words of John Barton, they need to "coin" or "fresh mint" the language.[27] Developing an attitude such as this toward the dialogue engenders a kind of game among the players and can result in a light tone of delivery.

Beckett was a careful crafter of language and his characters constantly search for and coin the best words to describe their existential situation. Accuracy in language and an obsession with poetic precision permeate the piece. Consider the story to which Hamm returns throughout the play. He begins a phrase only to stop, reconsider, and correct himself. Framing existence with precision is necessary because Hamm—like Beckett himself—is struggling to find the language which can encapsulate the numerous layers of his poetic vision. He's not after two birds with one stone; he's after a dozen. Ultimately, he finds language completely insufficient for expressing the unnameable. "There's English for you. Ah well."[28] Hamm consistently revises his "story" and he can't help but comment upon the efficacy of his expressions:

> HAMM: You prayed—
>
> (*Pause. He corrects himself.*)
>
> You CRIED for night; it comes—
>
> (*Pause. He corrects himself.*)
>
> It FALLS: now cry in darkness.
>
> (*He repeats, chanting.*)
>
> You cried for night; it falls: now cry in darkness.
>
> (*Pause.*)
>
> Nicely put, that.[29]

The other characters, too, shape, re-shape, and comment on their text. Clov searches for the right word to describe his kitchen and, once found, savors its deliciousness. "I'll go now to my kitchen, ten feet by ten feet by ten feet, and wait for him to whistle me. (*Pause.*) Nice dimensions, nice proportions."[30] Nagg is self-critical when referencing his delivery of the aforementioned story joke: "I never told it worse...I tell this story worse and worse."[31] Even old Nell bristles and corrects Nagg about his description of their ash bin litter: "Can you not be a little accurate, Nagg?"[32] The very performance of the characters becomes a topic as they selfreflect. "In the direct action of Endgame, there are constant comic references to the play as a play."[33] Their self-conscious struggle proves a tangible—even enjoyable—action for actors to play. "The dialogues coalesce in a playful form of self-reflexivity that borrows from the terminology of play-acting."[34] These copious allusions to performing in the theatre help the characters create a comic distance from their dire condition. "Certainly the comedy and the 'play' references [help] to undercut the reality of our dark inevitable situation where something is taking its course."[35]

Yet still, the dark and heavy content of the lines in *Endgame* can seduce actors into the trap of playing with a morose emotional attitude. This is understandable, given what the characters face, but the actors/characters must constantly look for ways to keep the emotional content at arm's length. They can do this by "fresh minting" words, exaggerating physically comic routines, acknowledging meta-theatrical references, leaning into the comic cadences of the text, and otherwise using comedy as a survival technique, for, as Alan Schneider points out, "humor is the bulwark against despair."[36]

Schneider, Beckett's foremost American director, went so far as to call the play "alternately terrifying and uproarious"[37] and claimed that the play "abounded with legitimate laughter."[38] Lightness of tone was evident in the 1957 production of Beckett's original French version, entitled Fin de Partie. This successful performance was universally cited for its humor. Harold Hobsen praised the "mordant humor" of George Adet's Nagg and the "wry" jokes of Jean Martin.[39] Jacques Lemarchand wrote that the "vigorous, savage" humor of the play provoked "brusque outbreaks of laughter."[40] Marc Bernard noted that the play "strangely resembles a parody" and shares its farcical tone with none other than Molière.[41]

Molière was heavily influenced by the troupes of Italian improvisers that toured through France in the 17th Century. He shared the theatre in the Palais Royale with Tiberio Fiorelli and it is said that he never missed a performance of the Italian.[42] Classic Commedia players used improvised comic business and extended physical set pieces in order to keep their audiences entertained. Generally, these audiences didn't understand Italian, so the players were pressed to engage them with sophisticated physical scenarios. These routines could be extremely elaborate, extending for several minutes. Clov's "ladder lazzi" in the opening sequence of the play can be traced back to Venice in the early 1600's, when Arlecchino's variations were documented by Flamino Scala.[43] These bits included the ladder sliding down a wall, shaking it, or using it like a pair of stilts. As performed by Max Cassela in the 2008 Andrè Belgrader production, Clov's dogged back and forth event became "a purely comic, silent-movie routine."[44] This sequence is cited by Duckworth, who notes:

> it is the physical comedy of Clov's stage business with the ladder and the flea-powder (like Lucky's with his impedimenta, and the three-hat routine of Didi and Gogo) that lightens the mood. However, it is in performance that such important visual elements can really be appreciated.[45]

Clov's flea-in-the-crotch business is related to lazzi enacted in Paris in 1674, in which Arlecchino contorted his body into countless difficult positions in an effort to catch an invisible, offending flea.[46] Clov's telescope bit, the long running joke of the painkiller, and the comic invention of the "wheelchair bit" are all derived from these classic routines. In the wheelchair sequence, the blind Hamm orders Clov to position him precisely in the center of the room:

CLOV: There!

(*pause*)

HAMM: I feel a little too far to the left.

(*Clov moves chair slightly.*)

Now I feel a little too far to the right.

(Clov moves the chair slightly.)

I feel a little too far forward.

(*Clov moves chair slightly*)

Now I feel a little too far back.

(*Clov moves chair slightly*)

Don't stay there.

(*i.e. behind the chair*)

You give me the shivers.

CLOV: If I could kill him I'd die happy.[47]

This routine is as predictable as it is fun. As frustrating as it is for the characters (and as morbid as Clov's punchline appears to be) the underlying format is that of a classic *Commedia* lazzi. This is vaudeville of the morgue—black humor—and the comic rhythm of these sections prevent the play from sinking into a pit of despair.

Attention to pace is critical to the success of the best productions of farce; so it is with *Endgame*. Beckett himself believed the overall tempo of the play should be upbeat. In 1967, he told a German Clov that "you should never run slowly, that's very dangerous for the play.[48] As noted earlier, the underlying pace and musical rhythm is reminiscent of classic stand-up duos and music hall comedy. Though the patter may not reach the clip of Didi and Gogo's repartee, "one of the primary realities," said Chaikin "is the vaudeville team, keeping the audience amused in this play about inertia and despair and deadendness [sic]."[49] When Frank Galati successfully directed Ian Barford as Clov at Steppenwolf Theatre in 2010, the actor "heightened and stylized his performance," imbuing the role with the energy of a "vaudevillian clown."[50]

The spirit of vaudeville and the British music hall lives on in the classic rhythm of set-ups and punchlines that are punctuated by a supporting drummer's double thump to the tom-tom and a crash of the symbol. One can almost hear a drummer's "rimshot" at the end of the following exchanges. Note the set-ups and punchlines:

HAMM: Why don't you kill me?

CLOV: I don't know the combination to the cupboard.[51]

. . . .

CLOV: I can't sit.

HAMM: True. And I can't stand.

CLOV: So it is.

HAMM: Every man his specialty.[52]

....

CLOV: "Do you believe in the life to come?"

HAMM: Mine was always that.[53]

....

CLOV: What's to keep me here?

HAMM: The dialogue.[54]

This is evidence of what Clurman coined "the special humor, the Beckett 'joke' which makes his work seem like a scenario for farce."[55] This is the sensibility which made critics swoon when Chaiken took his Manhattan Theatre Club production to Paris in 1980. He had "penetrated deep enough to find the laugh, the brutal burst of laughter."[56] To miss these rhythms is to miss not only the music of the moment, but the lightness that balances the darkness of the play.

In a letter to Alan Schneider on November 21, 1957, Beckett refers to a passage from pp. 58-61 of *Endgame* when he writes:

> 'Keep going, etc.' means 'keep asking me about my story, don't let the dialogue die.' Repeated ironically by Clov a little later with the same meaning. Cf. 'return the ball' in Godot. I think this whole passage—up to the recurrence of "end" motif—should be played as farcical parody of polite drawing-room conversation.[57]

The last lines of this directive from Beckett, underlined in his own hand, clearly indicate that performing Beckett requires the talents of actors well-versed in the art of verbal and physical comedy and that the characters are meant to "play ball" with each other. Understanding the forms of these games can help actors and directors lend cohesion and a sense of humor to a play that is far too often viewed through a very dark lens. Cohn's observation that "the play may be interpreted as a bitterly ironic version of creation and resurrection, making incidental use of comic devices, above all repetition"[58] does not go far enough to quantify the value of the play's underpinning. The comedy may be ironic, but is certainly not "incidental," as it is inextricably linked to its structure; for, according to Beckett himself, "what is said in [a work of art] is indissolubly linked with the manner in which it it is said."[59] This is why it is crucial to understand the humor in the bones of this play. Without it, a dreary nastiness dominates and the performers focus solely on the "cry" of the thing.

Hamm frequently acknowledges the "stand-up" nature of his relationship with Clov. He consciously draws attention to the jokes and routines they perform: "No phone calls? (*Pause*) Don't we laugh?"[60] No phone calls? It's an absurdly funny question to pose in a landscape such as this. Not only are there no phones, there's no electricity. There isn't anyone else to speak to. There's no one else, there's no where else. There's no more nature; there's no more tide; there's no more Turkish delight. There's no more pain-killer, decency, pap, or bicycle wheels.

Sawdust has been replaced with sand. Only the shards of jokes—and the odd flea—remain.

---

[1] Brater, Enoch. *Why Beckett.* Thames and Hudson Ltd., 1989, 83.

[2] Cohn, Ruby. *Samuel Beckett: The Comic Gamut.* Rutgers University Press, 1962, 325.

[3] Ibid., 228.

[4] Esslin, Martin. *The Theatre of the Absurd.* 3rd Edition, Random House, 2004, 406

[5] Ibid., 93

[6] Ibid., 22.

[7] Ibid.

[8] Beckett, Samuel. *Endgame.* Grove Press, 1958, 26.

[9] Ibid., 11.

[10] Ibid., 46.

[11] Ibid., 31.

[12] Ibid., 2.

[13] Ibid., 33.

[14] Ibid., 68.

[15] Clurman, Harold. "Review of *Endgame.*" *The Critical Response to Samuel Beckett.* Edited by Cathleen Culotta Andonian, Greenwood Press, 1998, 118.

[16] Bernard, Marc. "*Endgame.*" *Samuel Beckett: The Critical Heritage.* Edited by Lawrence Graver and Raymond Federman, Routledge and Kegan Paul, 1979, 167.

[17] Beckett, 14.

[18] Ibid., 78.

[19] Ibid., 81.

[20] Berlin, Normand. "Traffic of Our Stage: Beckett's *Endgame.*" *Massachusetts Review*, Vol. 50, Issue 3, 2009, 410.

[21] Brater, 78.

[22] Ibid., 84.

[23] Cohn, 234.

[24] Tynan, Kenneth. "*Endgame.*" *Samuel Beckett: The Critical Heritage.* Edited by Lawrence Graver and Raymond Federman, Routledge and Kegan Paul, 1979.164.

[25] Brater, 136.

[26] Beckett, 6.

[27] Barton, John. *Playing Shakespeare.* Methuen, 1986, 67.

[28] Beckett, 51.

[29] Ibid., 83.

[30] Ibid., 2.

[31] Ibid., 22.

[32] Ibid., 17.

[33] Cohn, 238.

[34] Morin, Emilie. "*Endgame* and Shorter plays: Religious, Political and Other Readings." *The New Cambridge Companion to Samuel Beckett*, edited by Dirk Van Hulle, Cambridge University Press, 2015, 67.

[35] Berlin, 411.

[36] Schneider, Alan. "Working With Beckett." *Chelsea Review*, Autumn, 1958, 188.

[37] Ibid., 180.

[38] Ibid., 185.

[39] Hobsen, Harold. "*Endgame.*" *Samuel Beckett: The Critical Heritage*. Edited by Lawrence Graver and Raymond Federman, Routledge and Kegan Paul, 1979, 164.

[40] Ibid., 170.

[41] Bernard, 167.

[42] Wilbur, Richard. "Introduction." *The School for Husbands*. Molière, translated by Richard Wilbur, Harcourt Brace Jovanovich, 1992, 1.

[43] Gordon, Mel. *Lazzi: The Comic Routines of the Commedia dell'Arte*. Performing Arts Journal Publications, 1983, 9.

[44] Berlin, 405.

[45] Duckworth, Colin. "Re-Evaluating *Endgame.*" *Dialogue*, Vol. 1, 2007, 26.

[46] Gordon, 12.

[47] Beckett, 27.

[48] Brater, 83.

[49] Ibid.

[50] Shanahan, Ann M. "*Endgame*: Theatrical Review." *Theatre Journal*, Johns Hopkins University Press, 62(3), 2010, 468.

[51] Beckett, 8.

[52] Ibid., 10.

[53] Ibid., 49.

[54] Ibid., 58.

[55] Clurman, 118.

[56] Brater, 84.

[57] Harmon, Maurice, ed. *No Author Better Served: The Correspondence of Samuel Becket and Alan Schneider*. Harvard University Press, 1998, 23.

[58] Cohn, 277.

[59] Esslin, 44.

[60] Beckett, 10.

PERFORMANCE REVIEWS

OKLAHOMA!. By Richard Rodgers and Oscar Hammerstein II. Directed by Daniel Fish. St. Ann's Warehouse, Brooklyn, NY, 31 October 2018.

Upon entering the raw, freshly constructed shell of a barn, audience members soon realize that this a very new *Oklahoma!*. Four long rows of wooden chairs flank either side of the rectangular performance space, a country-band tunes their instruments as the musicians engage in conversations, and an onstage table of corn awaits shucking. Streamers fly above the performance space, strings of party lights have been hung behind the audience, and crockpots sit on the wooden tables throughout the rustic, unfinished space. At one end of the barn, is a sepia-toned landscape of the Oklahoma farmland, and at the other end, a collage of rifles adorns the wall behind the band, a visual reminder of the violence that awaits at the end of this story. While the space is set for celebration, this production of *Oklahoma!* takes audiences on a very different journey.

Oklahoma! premiered on Broadway in 1943 amidst the violence and national unease of World War II. Based on the play *Green Grow the Lilacs* by Lynn Riggs, the musical marks the first collaboration between the seminal songwriting team of Richard Rodgers and Oscar Hammerstein II. Exploring the lives, romances, and troubles of Laurey, Curly, Jud, Ado Annie and Will Parker, part of the original success of *Oklahoma!* has been attributed to the musical's commentary on community and national identity during a time of war. Seventy-five years later, this production appears to be interested in highlighting another perspective of that story – the violence that humanity is capable of when that very community is threatened.

A reworking of a 2015 production presented at Bard SummerScape, this production serves as a scaled-down, more intimate version of *Oklahoma!* Under the imaginative direction of Daniel Fish and featuring new orchestrations and arrangements by Daniel Kluger, The St. Ann's Warehouse incarnation carefully examines the people of *Oklahoma!*, the complexity of their relationships and the human impact of their actions. Navigating the work as one of American drama, more so than as an

American musical, the acting company provides the work with a series of masterful performances: Damon Daunno's embodies Curly as a man that is both alluring and tremendously flawed; Rebecca Naomi Jones breathes new life into Laurey as a woman, coming of age, caught between two men, neither of whom she may love; Mary Testa's Aunt Eller is enacted with refreshing honesty, subtlety, and humor, providing *Oklahoma!* with a matriarch that is compassionate in some moments and cold in others. Standing out among this noteworthy field are two revelatory performances - Ali Stroker as Ado Annie and Patrick Vaill as Jud Fry. Stroker became the first actor in a wheelchair to appear on Broadway during the successful 2015 revival of *Spring Awakening*. In *Oklahoma*, Stroker continues to break new ground, embodying an Ado Annie that is not only sexually alive, but also boldly navigating her future with deceptive intelligence. As Jud Fry, Patrick Vaill provides a surprisingly vulnerable, sympathetic version of the character, one that is often interpreted as the villain of the musical, but instead is brought to life here as a wounded soul who is cruelly ostracized by the very community of which he seeks to be a part.

Although there have not been any narrative or textual revisions to the libretto of *Oklahoma!*, the revival has made some significant structural adjustments, all of which have been approved by the Rodgers and Hammerstein Organization. First, the now-famous dream ballet, which usually marks the end of Act I, now serves as the opening to Act II, giving the sequence new dramatic weight. Staged with strikingly revolutionary choreography by John Heginbotham, "Laurey Makes Up Her Mind" feels like Agnes de Mille choreography for the twenty-first century. Largely danced by a single dancer (the brilliant Gabrielle Hamilton), this dream ballet is nightmarish, abstract, confusing, and highly sexual, serving as a transformational window into the inner-life of Laurey. Second, beyond the placement and tone of the ballet, this revival also makes a large directorial (and narrative) revision in the death of Jud Fry. While specific details will be intentionally omitted here to preserve a sense of surprise for future audience members, the revision boldly reveals the blood on the hands of "Curly," "Laurey," "Aunt Eller," the community in the death of "Jud." Lastly, the size of the cast has been significantly pared-down to one of ten actors, and the large ensemble that is often associated with Rodgers and Hammerstein musicals has been mostly eliminated. Whereas the function of the ensemble has been important in earlier productions of the musical in order to represent the larger community in which the story takes place, in this production the role of the community is played by us, the audience, placing us not only within the action, but also asking us to question our role in the tragic events therein.

While perhaps more subtle and direct in its tone than other productions of the musical, this production succeeds at challenging, enlightening, and entertaining the audience. With audience lighting "on" for much of the performance, and chili and cornbread served to the audience at intermission, as the audience occupies the same wooden seats that the characters fill on stage, we – the audience – are part of this community. While the audience may have come to "see" a production of *Oklahoma!*, they are, in fact, being placed into the community of *Oklahoma!*, making them witness to, and to some extent, complicit in, the actions that unfold. Told with refreshing honesty, avoiding any overacting that is sometimes (incorrectly) associated with the musical theatre form, these characters speak, sing, dance, relate in the most familiar and human ways, creating an *Oklahoma!* that is both accessible and heartbreaking. Through reimagined music, choreography, direction and characters, this production of *Oklahoma!* asks audiences to also reimagine, to reconsider, our own actions, our communities, who is invited into those communities, who is kept on the outskirts, and the potentially violent ramifications therein.

RYAN MCKINNEY
Kingsborough Community College
The City University of New York

AMERICAN SON. By Christopher Demos-Brown. Directed by Kenny Leon. Booth Theatre, New York, New York, 4 January 2019.

Christopher Demos-Brown's Broadway play, *American Son*, is both relevant and poignant. Seemingly ripped from current headlines, *American Son* focuses on an estranged interracial couple awaiting news about their son whom they believed was involved in a police incident. As the couple waits for news of their son, they delve into issues of racism, sexism, racial identity, and parenting. Their conversations force audiences to question how racism and prejudice have woven their way into the fabric of America as we sit idly bye.

Miami-based playwright Christopher Demos-Brown is making his Broadway debut at the age of 54. His seemingly-late playwriting success is largely due to the fact that playwriting is his second job. Demos-Brown is a practicing lawyer in Miami with his wife and law partner Stephanie. Demos-Brown is not new to theatre, however, as he and his wife are founding members of the Miami-based theatre company Zoetic Stage. Demos-Brown's law background provides the impetus for this play of parental crisis and racial tension. Demos-Brown is a white playwright tackling the issue of race in America. He constructs a play as nuanced and complicated as the issue is in our country highlighting that race is not a stand-alone issue but is tied to and directly impacts all the ways in which people identify. Demos-Brown focuses on the intersection of race and marriage, gender, parenting, age and identity. Focusing on the universal topics that affect all people is what makes this play impactful. Although it may seem like too much to pack into one 90-minute show without intermission, director Kenny Leon manages to do it with intimacy and grit. Leon, Tony-winner for his direction of *A Raisin in the Sun* (2014), highlights the humanity in each character in this production, regardless of their divergent point of views.

The four-member cast is led by Golden-globe and Emmy nominated actress, Kerry Washington, months after the successful six-year run of the Shonda Rhimes' drama, *Scandal*. Washington delivers an emotionally raw performance in the role of college professor Kendra Ellis-Connor, the worried mother of Jamal, her 18-year old bi-racial son. As the curtain rises, the audience sees Kendra waiting alone in the Miami police station. Derek McLane's scenic design features large windows that illustrates Kendra's isolation by dwarfing her when she is alone on stage at the beginning of the play. McLane's seemingly simple set creates a quiet, cold, and sterile environment that traps Kendra and her estranged, white FBI agent husband Scott (normally played by Steven Pasquale, but at this performance was played by Brian Avers) in the confined space with no escape, driving them to their emotional limits. As the couple continues to wait for news about their son from a higher-ranking officer the mounting pressure, fear and anxiety begins to bring out the worst in the estranged couple. Kendra and Scott have a series of verbal sparring matches about their failed marriage, their perspectives on how to parent a bi-racial son the world only sees as a black man, and their differing understanding of racism, white privilege, and gender expectations.

As Malcom X said, "The most disrespected woman in America, is the Black Woman."[1] As an audience member with this knowledge and a grasp of recent current events one cannot help but empathize with Kendra's pursuit for news about her son. Kendra must work to have her voice, concerns, and questions heard and validated. It is no coincidence the voice of an African-American woman is fighting to be heard in this play. Kendra demands answers and respect from the young white rookie cop Paul Larkin, (played with ease by Jeremy Jordan), her husband, and Lieutenant Stokes. As a mother, she is in anguish and no one, not even Jamal's father can

---

[1] From what is colloquially known as the "Who Taught You to Hate Yourself" speech. Malcolm X delivered these words in 1962 in Los Angeles as part of a funeral service for Ronald Stokes, one of seven members of the Nation of Islam killed by police on April 27 of that year at their mosque in an altercation about the police department's recent activity of monitoring the mosque and its members.

understand: the fear an African-American mother feels for her son involved in an unspecified police incident with no answers or communication.

The most interesting interaction in this play is between the two African-American characters, Kendra and Lieutenant John Stokes, played powerfully by Eugene Lee. Stokes seems to be the only one capable of matching wits with Kendra. He is not afraid to use his power in the situation to restore order when he feels Kendra and Scott have gotten out of hand. Demos-Brown manages to subvert audience expectation when Stokes blames Kendra for her son's involvement in the incident. Earlier in the play, Scott revealed that Jamal placed a controversial bumper sticker on his car about police in the wake of deaths of unarmed black men like Eric Garner, Tamir Rice, and Philando Castile. Kendra and Stokes argue about how the next generation of African-Americans should behave, which is informed by how they were taught to act. Stokes believes in the path his generation took in which everyone was clean cut, well-mannered, and obedient to authority to ensure their survival. Kendra, however, raised Jamal to believe he has dignity, rights, and a voice to demand equality and justice. It is their disagreement that leaves the audience questioning if there is a prescribed set of behaviors for African-Americans to ensure their safety. How can they show their blackness is not a threat? It is the pondering of that question that reminds audience members of the sad reality of race relations in this country.

In the end, Stokes reveals the tragic news to Kendra and Scott that their son was killed in a police incident early that morning. Jamal is never seen or heard in this play, but news of his death manages to suck the oxygen from the theatre. Despite all the debates, conversations, and difference of perspectives, in the end a young, innocent boy is dead. Audiences are left with a small glimpse of the pain families who deal with this horror must feel. There is no silver lining, no hopeful undertone, just the sad reality that a life was lost. Demos-Brown's play seems to echo the sad and truthful words of Childish Gambino, "This is America."

AARON BROWN
Baylor University

KNEAD. Written and Performed by Mary Lynn Owen. Directed by David de Vries. Alliance Theatre, Atlanta, GA. 9 December 2018.

Watching a woman bake bread over the course of ninety minutes is bound to leave an audience a bit hungry, and Mary Lynn Owen's *Knead* at the Alliance Theatre in Atlanta left the audience desiring not only bread but also human connection. Owen presents a delicate tale of blurred memories and merged timelines against the backdrop of attempting, once again, to succeed with her mother's bread recipe. A flawed woman sharing the story of her equally flawed family, particularly her mother, in a narrative that exquisitely presents the muddled aspects of intangible memories delivers a powerful experience that results in a theatrical communion amongst the audience.

The work was originally developed as a project in 3rd Reiser Atlanta Artists Lab and was a 2017 semi-finalist for the O'Neill National Playwright's Conference. *Knead*'s world premiere at the Alliance Theatre features the playwright performing herself in this autobiographical one-woman show. *Knead* opens with Mary Lynn Owen already on stage as the audience enters. She is looking curiously at a worn piece of paper that has been lovingly tended over the years, repaired with tape and stained with culinary attempts. The audience later learns this is her mother's bread recipe and she has attempted to make it many times always to what she feels are disastrous results, never quite getting it right. The recipe itself becomes a catalyst for Mary's trip down memory lane. Owen navigates the challenges of an autobiographical work with her warmth and welcome to the audience to share in her memories. The vulnerability she expresses, and openness to honestly confront the memories she encounters, lulls the audience into feeling like a comfortable guest in Owen's home. Her use of well-timed comedy helps to diffuse moments that might be overwhelmingly tragic.

Rather than mire itself in realistic retellings of memories, *Knead* embraces the fractured inspirations of recollection by offering up magical moments of finding tangible memories in the oddest places around Owen's kitchen. At one point as she moves around collecting ingredients and supplies she opens her refrigerator, utters a surprised exclamation, climbs in the fridge extracting a tricycle. This moment spurs stories of her challenging brother who continually pulled the attention of her parents. In another example, Owen opens a drawer for a pot but instead finds her long lost 4-H vest prompting her recollections of her first attempt to make flan. When pink 'Breast Cancer Awareness' paraphernalia flies out unexpectedly from a cabinet she shares the tragic story of her double mastectomy that turned out to be unnecessary. These moments remind us that our lives are constantly shifting between the now and the then, as well as converging between the two points, and that no matter the literal progression of time, our actions and choices do not necessarily follow a continuum but are sometimes pushed off track by unexpected moments or memories.

Fig. 1. Mary Lynn Owen in *Knead*, Alliance Theatre. Photo by Greg Mooney. Used by Permission.

Owen's play confronts the assumption of life that there is a recipe, that if one only follows the directions, one will find success. The audience watches the bread rest and rise, they see her measure the ingredients precisely, and watch as she kneads the dough with strength and determination. The bread recipe counters the imprecision of life with the precision of ingredients and technique. Her own experiences as a Cuban-American and Methodist pastor's daughter in rural Georgia, (her recipe), is so specific but at the same time she is able to connect more broadly to the audience. In the end she bakes bread that is misshapen, but as she cuts it open before us, it steams and smells just like any tasty bread. This is a metaphor for our own lives as we are often "misshapen" by life but our lives are just as worthy and important as any other. Just as she wrestles with the memory of her baking-obsessed mother who she notes never quite fit in the "right box," Owen discovers that there really is no box, just shapes of all sorts. There is a clear sense of a desire to connect further with her roots while also proclaiming her own unique identity as she struggles to mimic her mother's breadmaking. The play presents the joys, failures and despair that life brings, but these are always balanced skillfully and delicately by Mary Lynn Owen's performance and David de Vries' direction. Owen's writing is also to be commended as she carefully navigates her autobiographical story cleverly excluding parts of her timeline and many details about her life, but the stories she has chosen to share interweave to form a lovely design in the end.

Knead is a particularly important show for our current world as it reminds us of the importance of hearing and sharing our own unique stories. Owen keeps the audience aware of their own presence by referring directly to them every so often during the course of the play, clearly breaking the fourth wall amidst a wonderfully detailed and realistic kitchen set. The audience are not voyeurs peeking in, but they are welcome guests as she struggles to tell the audience her story. Furthermore, the immersive scent of baking bread surrounds the audience for much of the play making it almost impossible not to feel directly involved in this moment or that we are not in fact sitting in a kitchen.

Knead celebrates community and empathy and encourages its audience to break bread and tell stories. Owen seems to come to terms with her memories and a form of reconciliation is achieved. By searching her memories to find her identity she finally owns her individuality and heritage by the end of the show. In the final moment of the play, after tasting her bread, which finally passes muster, she looks out towards the audience, her face filling with joy and exclaims, "It was you!" The labor of the breadmaking and the audience's attention to her story ends the performance on a triumphant note further emphasizing the communion experience of the show as pieces of the baked loaf are offered in the lobby as the audience leaves.

CHRISTINE SUSTEK WILLIAMS
Lee University

THE MAGIC NEGRO AND OTHER BLACKITY BLACKNESS AS TOLD BY AN AFRICAN AMERICAN MAN WHO ALSO HAPPENS TO BE BLACK. Written and performed by Mark Kendall. Cleveland Play House, Outcalt Theatre. May 18 2019.

With humor and total boldness in a solo performance with a multitude of characters Mark Kendall brings complexity, depth and brilliant execution to his play *The Magic Negro and Other Blackity Blackness*. Mark Kendall is an Atlanta Native, whose piece was part of The New Ground Theatre 2019 festival at Cleveland Play House in Cleveland, Ohio.

The titular character, The Magic Negro, escorts us through the production. He is the embodiment of a deeply familiar archetype: the black wise man that leads the white man into discovering that everything he needed was already inside of him. He is Nick Fury in *The Avengers*, Morpheus in *The Matrix*, Future in *8 Mile*. He is most characters that Morgan Freeman has played. He is recognizable because he has become a staple in the entertainment industry, a recognizable archetype deeply rooted in the American collective storytelling.

Every single moment in this sketch comedy play is meaningful, deeply political and resonates with the current and historical American landscape. Mark Kendall is not afraid to throw punches, and he is not modulating his performance to cater to anyone. According to the Broadway League in 2017-2018 "The vast majority of Touring Broadway theatregoers were Caucasian"[2] And this was not the exception during this particular performance. Regardless of this, *The Magic Negro and Other Blackness* brought a good amount of black and brown audience members to the New Ground Theatre Festival. The Magic Negro, our host for the night, embraces the differences of its audience members without excusing them. We have been invited into his space, and he is going to take us on a journey. He understands the demographics of his audience and he is not antagonizing anyone, instead he creates an inclusive atmosphere by speaking the radical truth of the way things are.

Kendall most successfully interacts with the white audience members when he is trying illuminate the difficulties of interacting with other racial groups. For instance: he invites an audience member to participate in an obstacle course which reflects the struggles that black people live with everyday under capitalism in America. Imagine this: a white and a black boy are together in the obstacle course. In this case the audience member a white man is the black boy. Then just as he is starting the race he gets hit by the first obstacle which is slavery. At that moment he needs to go back to the beginning of the course. Then as it appears that he is advancing he gets hit by multiple aggressions that black people are victim to daily such as segregation, cultural appropriation and so on.

He also examines issues like white guilt. In one sketch Kendall takes on the role of a white man and asks himself to list the five greatest male actors. The list starts with Matt Damon and Ryan Gosling ("The Savior of Jazz"), and by number four he notices he has not included a black actor. He starts to look for a male black actor in his memory so people do not think he is racist. And within this mental dilemma, Kendall morphs into the character of white guilt which slowly and painfully comes to the seating area and address the audience fiercely. He reminds them of decisions they have made powered by white guilt instead of from a genuine place. The character of White Guilt collapses at the feet of a random white audience member in the first row who is asked to read from a "To-do" list. This list varies from "I will never touch a black person's hair" to "Give *Atlanta* (the TV show) a try." In the end Kendall morphs back to naming the five greatest male actors yet his final choice is still Chris Pine.

Among many other sketches the heaviest one is perhaps the premise of being "Beyoncé on a plantation". After donning a blond wig and sitting cross legged, Mark Kendall breaks character. He takes a pause and mentions that he will not continue to portray his culture for the sake of a laugh, asking how can he make someone feel comfortable laughing at a topic that has never brought him comfort. Therefore, he

---

[2] [Report] Broadway League, "The Audience for Touring Broadway 2017-2018 SEASON," 2019 February.

decides to make something unfunny for a change. Out of his pocket, he pulls the Cookie Monster's shopping list, and it is just what one would expect; only cookies. As he lists, "cookies, cookies, cookies, cookies" endlessly, louder and louder, Kendall begins throwing Oreos into the audience, which triggers Kendall to morph into the Cookie Monster himself. With just a hat and the iconic Cookie Monster voice Kendall shares an incredible message: that Kendall is just like the Oreos he is throwing at the audience. He is black on the outside but on the inside he is still perpetuating white supremacy, a reality that every person of color struggles with. Kendall questions how from our own trenches we continue to be involved in the colonial project, giving power to the white sentiment that white is better, white is the norm. To wrap up and to find some calm he again invites a random white member of the audience on stage with him to see if both can become friends despite their differences. Kendall asks him some questions such as "Do you support slavery?" Then during three full minutes of the Reading Rainbow's theme song both men make deep eye contact, and become friends while holding hands.

The Magic Negro and Other Blackity Blackness is a great reminder that people can talk to each other honestly and safely, if the right circumstances are set for a safe exchange of relevant information. The piece brings us on journey, reminding us that every black person is different, complex and unique, and at the same time deeply affected by the system that has made it a goal to oppress black people. This strikingly relevant, provocatively funny play continues to tour in different parts of the United States.

JULIA ROSA SOSA
University of Texas, El Paso

AN OCTOROON. By Branden Jacobs-Jenkins. Directed by Akin Baba-tunde. Stage West Theatre, Fort Worth, TX. 2 & 30 September 2018.

Branden Jacobs-Jenkins's play opens with a monologue—actually a dialogue delivered by one actor—in which a "black playwright" named BJJ recreates a conversation he never had with a therapist who doesn't exist. The (non-existent) therapist presses BJJ to identify "any playwrights who you admire." Insofar as an enactment of a phantasm is entitled to expectations, hers point to some generic exemplar of Blackness, perhaps, one imagines, the gal who wrote that musical, *Raisin*. But BJJ responds with a surprising admission masked as an interrogative: "Dion Boucicault?" The (bewildered) therapist confesses ignorance of the popular nineteenth-century Irish-American melodramatist and of the play—*The Octoroon*—that BJJ names. "And you . . . like this play?" "Yes."

In the 2 September 2018 performance of Stage West's remarkable production, the preposterously talented Ryan Woods voiced this affirmation with a bemused lilt, as if to suggest that BJJ hadn't much pondered the matter but was pleased to own an eccentric enthusiasm. By the closing matinee on 30 September, Woods was barking out the monosyllable: *yes*, dammit, I like that play. The production's run thus moved toward a fuller assertion of what I take to be this play's animating truth: Jacobs-Jenkins loves melodrama. His play gleefully exposes the reflexive racism of Boucicault's 1859 triumph while celebrating its ambient radicalism and reveling in its artifice. The tableaux, asides, and declamatory speeches—and set designer Bob Lavellee's scenic drops—are acts of homage, enlivened in this production with an irony too sinuous and nimble to be mistaken for parody.

Lavallee's decision to open with a ghost light illuminating a sparse stage is therefore both witty and wise. Like Suzan-Lori Parks's *Venus*, this play loves the work that haunts it—not only *The Octoroon* but also Eugene O'Neill's *Hairy Ape*, Spike Lee's *Bamboozled*, and Mel Brooks's *Blazing Saddles*, surely the inspiration for the bravura knife fight between BJJ and M'Closky, both played by Woods, sporting a laterally contrastive suit designed by Aaron Patrick DeClerk. When the ghost light blinks off at prologue's end, the Boucicault-Jacobs-Jenkins mash-up begins. Enter Ghost(s).

An Octoroon is a play within a play. The constituent plays are integrated in the manner of Buckingham's *The Rehearsal* and Frayn's *Noises Off*, as distinct from the more neatly partitioned precedents like *A Midsummer Night's Dream* and *Hamlet*. Passages adopted from and taken verbatim from Boucicault's play jostle against the playwright-adaptor's own street-slangy set pieces. Presented as melodramatic asides, even these last bits honor the play's generic origins. In both performances that I saw, the audience relished the collision of hip and often salty talk and a presentation that is both "corny" and, in its built-in solicitousness, generous.

Part of the fun involves the comings, goings, and permutations of BJJ and his furious, sottish counterpart The Playwright (Boucicault, in effect, played with frightening intensity by Justin Duncan). Having introduced in a prologue the plays that will play within their play, BJJ and The Playwright disappear, although the actors linger as the stock hero George and the villain M'Closky (Woods/BJJ), and the Indigene Wahnotee and the auctioneer LaFouche (Duncan/The Playwright). They return in act 4 to explain the source-play's machinery, meaning both the mechanisms of plot and the machine—the camera that records Wahnotee's murder—on which plot turns in Boucicault's original. The revenant playwrights have thematic work to do as well. BJJ yields to, or "becomes," George, who denounces the mob that would lynch the innocent Wahnotee. George's sincere speech about vigilantes "thirsting for . . . blood" wants to cut to the quick but, melodrama being melodrama, can't—yet. Prompted by his doppelganger BJJ, George again delivers his oration, this time, at least in Jacobs-Jenkins's script, with a "lynching photograph [projected] on the back wall." That works, or would have worked had not Lavellee's set fallen short in this one instance. His medley of sketched images—a cross, a hood, a tumbling, inverted body, oddly Keith Herring-ish—favored stylized tact where the playwright had called for bluntness. The lax, noosed ropes hanging from the flies at rise would seem to have recommended closer fidelity to Jacobs-Jenkins's instructions at this later point. We needed tautening here, not retreat.

Prominent among the challenges that this play stands to face in regional markets is a shortage of actors trained to perform as their great-grandparents might have done. Like playing farce and the bass guitar, playing melodrama is often regarded as something that one can do easily by virtue of doing something related fairly well. This is bunk, of course, and director Babatunde scores big by honoring overt artifice as an aesthetic category with its own formal and dramaturgical demands. Woods's M'Closky menaces here as the character must have done in 1859, inspiring, as Duncan's Playwright does, the down-market version of fear and pity on which melodrama depends. Nikki Cloer's soubrette, Dora, snaps her fan and tosses her curls as artfully as any predecessor could have done. Only the would-be ingenue, Zoe (Morgana Wilborn), succumbs to unalloyed sincerity, perhaps because the type she plays demands a reserve hostile to the exuberance that characterizes this production.

Several actors cast as slaves modulate athletically between the stylization demanded by genre and the now-speak sections that deliver humor and alienation. ("I worry about the whole thing becoming too Brechtian," Jacobs-Jenkins muses in a textual note; "though, does it matter?") Kristen White and Bretteney Beverly sync perfectly as new BFF's Minnie and Dido, particularly when they speak as no character in any nineteenth-century melodrama ever spoke. "Who ghetto now, bitch?!" perhaps clunks in a review but kills when Beverly flings it at the nasty, hapless house-slave Grace (Camille Monae), previously critical of the former field hand Minnie but now humbled by her own sale to M'Closky.

As George's re-contextualized oration suggests, meta isn't always funny in *An Octoroon*. DeClerk costumed the kowtowing slave Pete (Christopher Llewyn Ramirez) in the trappings of minstrelsy: outsized white gloves, exaggerative blackface, and a huge matted wig, all the while bawling ejaculations like "laws-a-mussey." Thus accoutered, Ramirez coaxed laugh after laugh from the audience, myself and my companions included. In the penultimate scene, however, Ramirez does his shtick sans wig—a jarring, potent move not suggested by the script. Pete suddenly looks like a cherubic actor. His debasement rebukes Boucicault, momentarily accenting the agonism present in any intelligent adaptation, however fond.

Br'er Rabbit (Christopher Lew) wanders on and off stage, providing an uncomfortable circumambience. He closes the play by walking down a denuded stage toward the audience, describing a circle with the tomahawk and gavel he holds, counterpoised. The symbol is easy to appreciate but resists precise application. This seems an apt metaphor for Jacobs-Jenkins's dazzling play, as realized by an exceptionally skillful team.

ALEXANDER PETTIT
University of North Texas

TÓMAS AND THE LIBRARY LADY. By José Cruz González. Adapted from the book by Pat Mora. Directed by Alicia Lark Fuss. Nashville Children's Theatre, 8 May 2019.

The 2018-2019 Nashville Children's Theatre season concluded with the company's first bilingual production since inception in 1931, ending an eighty-eight-year trend of English-dominated theatre. Director Alicia Lark Fuss and her production team presented *Tomás and the Library Lady* by José Cruz González, which is based on Pat Mora's children's book, which recounts the story of Tomás, the young son of Mexican-American migrant workers. Each summer, Tomás and his family must leave Texas to work in Iowa at the expense of Tomás's education. One year, Tomás discovers a local Iowan library, and with the help of the librarian, quickly increases in language and literacy skills.

Mora's book is based on the authentic story of Mexican-American author and educator Tomás Rivera (1935-1984), a child of migrant farm workers who discovered libraries at a young age. Despite hardships, Rivera earned four post-secondary degrees, including a PhD in Romance Languages and Literature from the University of Oklahoma. He taught at Sam Houston State University and the University of Texas at San Antonio before achieving Vice President of the University of Texas at El Paso and Chancellor of the University of California. Rivera authored several short stories, poems, and scholarly works, as well as the novel *...y no se lo tragó la tierra,* for which he received the Premio Quinto Sol literary award in 1971.

The Nashville Children's Theatre's one-hour production of *Tomás and the Library Lady* opened with the curtain speech in both English and Spanish, setting up an unapologetic tone that the play would flow between the two languages. With Nashville's immigration rate doubling over the last ten years, the company's play selection represented an inclusive gesture to the community, and an acknowledge-ment of the changing demographics of the city. A chief issue in American politics today, immigration serves as a valuable topic to explore on the stage. The play retains the light-hearted quality of Theatre for Young Audiences, never going over the heads of its young patrons, yet not masking the challenges and discrimination foreign-born Americans face.

The play begins with Tomás and his family working the fields of Texas, and his parents' announcement that they will be leaving for Iowa immediately. As they travel, Tomás experiences nightmares of an American teacher punishing him for not speaking English correctly, and is apprehensive for his new life in a different state. He and his family speak Spanish almost exclusively. As the family settles into the hard work of midwestern farming, Tomás's grandfather, Papa Grande, regales the family with stories each night. Papa Grande discovers Tomás knows every word of his stories and encourages him to find a library to learn new ones. Tomás is fearful of the over-sized Carnegie Library, which he mistakes for a meat shop as "carne" means "meat" in Spanish. The librarian, an older German woman, helps him

Fig 2. Matthew Benenson Cruz ("Tómas") and Rona Carter ("The Library Lady") in *Tómas and the Library Lady*, Nashville Children's Theatre. Photo by Michael Scott Evans. Used by permission.

navigate the new world of books, and Tomás quickly takes to reading and telling stories of his own.

For this production, Rona Carter (Storyteller 1) alternated between Tomás mother, brother, and the librarian, while Matthew Beneson Cruz (Storyteller 2) played both Tomás and his father. Referring to the characters as "storytellers" reflects a Brechtian nature to the play, which the production team enhanced with a scenic design that remained permanent as the play locations shifted. Even as the story began in Texas fields, a library with books and shelves remained on the stage, and the title of the play hovered overhead in large red letters. Chairs in various configurations represented cars and benches, while costume pieces hung on pegs on the stage, allowing the actors to change aprons, jackets, and hats in full view of the audience. Simple props and vocal changes translated character and location shifts, and effective projections aided the effort.

Keeping the production simple and focused allowed the audience to stay engaged in a way that would have been undone by excess blackouts, scenic changes, and actor exits. The static nature of the library framed the story and heightened the unchanging power of literacy. The library is always there, waiting to be discovered. For first- and second-generation Hispanic immigrant audience members, the production acknowledged their stories, and invited them into a theatre speaking their language for the first time. For English-speaking audiences, the play reminded them that education is for all. In the end, audience members cheered together after Tomás's final song, "Libros," in which he celebrated his new-found freedom through books.

Tomás and the Library Lady is well-suited to the canon of children's theatre works as it is relevant to America's growing immigration population today, and the element of bilingualism captures the tension of living between two worlds. Do all voices matter? The play says both "yes" and "sí."

BEKI BAKER
Lipscomb University

BOOK REVIEWS

LATINX THEATER IN THE TIMES OF NEOLIBERALISM. By Patricia A. Ybarra. Northwestern University Press, 2018. 264 pp. $34.95. Paperback.

Throughout *Latinx Theater in the Times of Neoliberalism*, Patricia Ybarra wants her readers to remember the real-life ramifications of neoliberal philosophies. The dedication to her book reads "For Berta Cáceres y los 43 de Ayotzinapa," citing two instances of fatal violence caused by the raging free market economy and privatization of the public sphere seen in Latin America. Each chapter features discussions of neoliberalism's consequential victims, from Cuban *balseros* and indigenous activists to "narcoguerra" militants and the murdered women of Juarez. Even a year after its publication, reality proves the necessity of this book: caravans of immigrants seeking refuge journey northward toward the United States' border, sparking outrage, compassion, and headlines across the Western Hemisphere. While the audience of this book may be traditional American theatre and humanities scholars and the students thereof, Ybarra wrote this book for this other audience—the immigrants, the victims, the survivors.

According to the Preface, Ybarra's journey with this book began when she was working on a play concerning those affected by Latinx neoliberal policies. She asked herself, "How exactly does one stage the destruction and denigration caused by savage capitalism in the wake of the demise of the U.S. social welfare state and the move to free-market economies throughout the hemisphere?" To answer this question, Ybarra dives into several plays by "transnational" writers and theatre makers. The author uses "transnational" in a broad sense: all of these artists actively practice theatre in U.S. markets while at the same time being conscious of their Latinx heritage, transcending national borders within their playmaking even when not physically crossing the border. Ybarra also acknowledges that some of these writers were born and raised in the United States but are still deeply connected to the political and economic climate of their ancestral countries.

After the Introduction, each chapter of Ybarra's book considers different phenomena resulting from the practices of neoliberal economics and several theatre pieces which attempt to display these consequences. While many of these phenomena overlap in time, Ybarra attempts to place them in chronological order, beginning with a chapter on NAFTA and the foundations of economic neoliberalism across the Americas. Specifically, this chapter examines plays which engage indigeneity and Western theatre tradition to comment on the imperial nature of neoliberal practices. The second chapter explores plays regarding the 1994 Cuban *Balseros* Crisis, where Cuban citizens attempted to flee the horrific economic conditions of their home country by rafting across the Florida Straits, only to be sent back home. Chapter Three investigates the free-market business practices in the maquiladora factories along the U.S./Mexico border and the effect these fast-expanding communities have on the female population. Since NAFTA, the rate of femicides in places like Ciudad Juarez has skyrocketed, creating a perilous environment for laboring women. Ybarra's last chapter focuses on the drama of narcotrafficking, ironically considering how the perpetrators of this trans-American drug trade exemplify the entrepreneurial principles of neoliberal philosophy.

Ybarra creates an atmosphere of ease throughout her text as she discusses decid-edly uneasy topics. The author structures her contentions with clarity, offering her readers an argument that builds with natural flow. Ybarra skillfully weaves together historical evidence with play analysis, crafting cogent answers to her book's main question. I find the most compelling theoretical discussion Ybarra asserts centers on the titular "Times of Neoliberalism." The author heavily examines the temporal structure of her chosen play texts, invoking J. Jack Halberstam's "queer time" as a parallel to the experience of individuals under the economic and political strictures of neoliberalism. The plays chosen for each chapter not only discuss the same neoliberal Latinx phenomenon, but also feature similar temporal structures. For example, the plays about the Cuban *balseros* feature temporalities of stagnation. Ybarra argues these people are stuck in an impasse; just as Cuba was not allowed to linearly progress because of economic embargos, neither were these characters. Discussions of eschatology, seriality, and recursivity populate the other chapters, signifying the deleterious effects of neoliberal economies on human progression and development.

To conclude her book, Ybarra pits the plays she has examined against the most popular immigrant story currently on the Broadway stage: Lin-Manuel Miranda's *Hamilton*. While she praises Miranda's motives for creating the hip-hop juggernaut, she finds the musical's views on Latinx transnationalism and politics to be problem-atic. She specifically cites Miranda's lack of examination on the relationship between liberalism and capitalism in colonial America, as well as the veneration of the "male immigrant entrepreneur" in American history. Ybarra contends that this master narrative continues to influence U.S. attitudes toward contemporary Latinx immigrants, once again reminding her readers of neoliberalism's insidious reality. In the end, Ybarra's goal is the same as that of the playwrights she examines: for audiences "up here" to not forget the recent violent history wrought by neoliberal policies "down there."

ZACH DAILEY
Texas Tech University

MEMORY, TRANSITIONAL JUSTICE, AND THEATRE IN POSTDICTATORSHIP ARGENTINA. By Noe Montez. Southern Illinois University Press, 2017. 262 pp. $45.00. Paperback.

As artists and scholars, we often hope that our work will carry weight beyond its immediate audience. In times of social and political unrest, especially when the government seems beyond reproach, we desire for our work to have a measurable effect on national thought and national policy. Noe Montez's *Memory, Transitional Justice, and Theatre in Postdictatorship Argentina* examines how Argentinian theatre, as sites of political engagement and social activism, intervenes in state-generated transitional justice practices. His work explores how Argentinian theatre challenges national policies, sometimes shaping the development of new laws and practices. Focusing on post-1989 Buenos Aires, Montez provides critical insight into multi-generational engagements with post-dictatorship "processes of producing memory" in Argentina since the Process of National Reorganization ended (4). In each chapter, Montez recounts major social and political policies and practices concerning memory narratives, followed by detailed descriptions and analyzes of theatrical events that engaged with or challenged those practices.

In the introduction, Montez clearly explains the parameters of this work. The plays discussed in the book are limited to productions and creators that originate in Buenos Aires and that are accessible to international audiences through tours or other media. Montez also provides an overview of Argentine theatre scholarship, political history, and memory studies. I found these explanations valuable because my previous work provided little context to understand the complexities of Argentina politics and the work of Argentinian theatre creators. This overview of the political and theatrical history of Argentina during and post Argentina's dictatorship prepares readers for Montez's chief claim: under the right circumstances, when activists' and the government's goals are aligned, "it is possible to produce memory narratives that grant legitimacy to transitional justice policies" (4).

Each chapter uses the featured productions to examine one facet of the relationship between collective memory and state policy. The first chapter examines Carlos Menem's move from state impunity to amnesty through reconciliation and "forgetting" the horrors committed under the dictatorship. The move toward reconciliation was countered by narratives in experimental productions, highlighting Argentina's many discourses on collective memory.

Where the first chapter explores personal narratives as a counterpoint to state-sponsored narratives, the second chapter explores the limits of personal narratives. Primarily, this chapter seeks to prove that the works highlighted in the first chapter "shifted the national memory narratives away from acceptance of the Menem administration's policies of impunity/amnesty and toward a desire to see the disappearances redressed" (62). Montez examines human rights activists' emphasis on the collection of archival evidence (such as genetic information from human remains) as a means to advocate for justice, as well as the pursuit of judicial measures to bring closure to the families of the disappeared and prevent these atrocities in the future.

Montez further examines the notion "reconciliation and forgetting" in documenting how the Grandmothers of the Plaza de Mayo—a human rights organization dedicated to finding children illegally adopted during the dictatorship and returning them to their biological families—collaborated with theatre artists in 2000 to create *Teatroxlaidentidad,* an organized framework for creating political theatre and social justice theatre. Particularly compelling in the chapter is Montez's analysis of why and how the Grandmothers prioritize "data over personal anecdotes," especially when discussing the kidnapped children of the disappeared (73). *Teatroxlaidentidad* performances mirror The Grandmothers' priorities by providing a counterpoint to established post-dictatorship theatre practices of privileging individual recollection over evidence.

The third chapter focuses on the policies enacted during the Nestor Kirchner administration, which included reversing the policies and practices of impunity and amnesty and calling for nationwide responsibility of violence during the dictatorship. Montez notes that Kirchner even impeached several supreme court justices and fired several high-ranking military officials. As these changes occurred in Argentina's presidency, military, and judiciary, Argentina's theatre narratives also changed. Montez explains that that contemporary theatre practitioners were children during the dictatorship, and their work combined memory narratives on identity with accounts of the way that archival materials and new technologies informed their understanding of identity. While these works appear less political than the work of the previous generation, Montez argues that these works are important step in Argentina's need to self-document the long-lasting effects of the Process and dictatorship. Additionally, works from this period establish Argentina as a leader in navigating transitional justice, using theatre in a "meaningful role in the process of memorialization" (146).

In the fourth chapter, Montez shifts to alternative, and often complicated and conflicted, narratives of military veterans from the dictatorship. As the government's position on impunity/amnesty changed and the public aged, the public's relationship to the military also changed. This chapter concludes with an overview of political issues in Argentina since 2013. Particularly of note is the Macri administration's work to reverse the human rights centered policies of the Kirchner administration, once again leading theatre to create memory narratives that complicate and resist official political perspectives and policy.

While I am hesitant to accept that the theatre of Buenos Aires speaks for all of Argentina, Noe Montez's careful curation and close examination of both Argentina's post-dictatorship politics and the theatre of Buenos Aires transcends the typical historiography—becoming a case study on theatre's ability to act as a catalyst in political change and a facilitator in creating collective memory narratives. Additionally, Montez's work on the intersections of memory, performance, and activism may be of interest to scholars studying other sites of post-violence and political upheaval, as well as theatre's potential role in other areas of social justice and political activism.

JENNIFER EZELL
Texas Tech University

THEATRE AND CARTOGRAPHIES OF POWER: REPOSITIONING THE LATINA/O AMERICAS. Edited by Jimmy A. Noriega and Analola Santana. Southern Illinois University Press, 2018. 320 pp. $60.00. Paperback.

Encapsulating the Latin American experience is a daunting task, even when winnowed to focus on an historical examination of prominent theatrical activity. Thankfully, the editors of *Theatre and Cartographies of Power* approach their attempt by situating "Latino/as" as a conjunction of races, beliefs, and identities, with diffuse but strong ties of language, history and yearnings—a social group whose imprint moves all over, from Canada to Tierra del Fuego. This edited collection attempts to (re)view theatre through an inverted framework of power dynamics, with particular interest in the means by which geography delimitates different power relations between diverse actors. The editors and contributors want to critique the way traditional positions over geographical divisions have arbitrarily organized the approach to scholarship, as well as the way spaces of power and knowledge have been created in realpolitik and recreated on stage.

The first clue to the depth of the editors' awareness of these multivalent issues is the title of the collection itself, which serves as a code where the stakes of the cont(in)ent can be interpreted. This also helps frame the book and its goals within a particular theoretical approach in regards to the curation of the scholarship present in the study. The new cartographies proposed in this text looks for a re-mapping of the study of these subjects on inquiry—through the metaphor of an upside map of the American continent, first visualized in 1936 by Uruguayan artist Joaquín Torres-García's *America Invertada*. This notion of the "south-up map" underscores a frequent and uniting theme of the collection: that Latin America is the place where knowledge can be created, but also the place that can be repositioned to provide a new categorization and organization of that knowledge.

Looking for a scholarly position of the study, the editors go beyond a literary review of their sources, creating a whole genealogy of scholarship concerning Latin Americans' historiographical and critical approach to texts, performances, and methods of production. It is clear this collection follows the work of Diana Taylor and Juan Villegas' "Negotiating Performance: Gender, Sexuality, and Theatricality in the Latin/o Americas," but the editors also chart their own course through examining the enormous corpus of Latin American theatre and performance. By using Torres-García inverted map as a metaphor, the collection is able to rediscover the works of significant figures as Enrique Buenaventura, Augusto Boal, Colectivo Cuatrotablas, Teatro Escambray, or Teatro Campesino. With these great theatre-makers evoked, the collection then guides us forward into new uncharted territory over a vast group of options to study and analysis, introducing new Latina/o creations from all over the continent. It seems to be a priority of the editors to highlight how this new cartography—studying the Latina/o phenomenon of theatrical reation in the U.S.—reinforces just how ephemeral real political borders are.

On the surface, the book is divided into five different parts: 1) Crafting Theoretical Frameworks from beyond the U.S. Borders, 2) Rethinking Histories of Geography, 3) The Historical Body: Race and Ethnicity, 4) Rewriting the Nation: Theatrical Methodology and Experimentation, and 5) Theatre in Motion: Global Networks and Production Practices. Yet, in order to create different ways to teach theatre and performance of, and from, Latin America in U.S. academe, the collection ultimately creates a new map of organization, where different voices talking about the creation and scholarship produced by Latina/os, and how that affects the power relations over society. The scholarship in Latin America comes from a different tradition than the scholarship in the United States, and the editors not only understand this, but they accommodate the book in a way all these different voices can be understood in their context and their aspirations.

To achieve those goals, the collection takes a very eclectic path, by proposing a dialectic relation between U.S. experts in Latin American artistic creation, Latina/o scholars from Latin American academia, and the voices and reflections of artists and creators (performers, playwrights, and directors). This enmeshed approach puts together an ambitious variety of voices, without falling prey to a traditional hierarchy—the collection does feature U.S. scholars that work and understand the Latina/o condition as Jorge Huerta, Diana Taylor and Brian Eugenio Herrera, but also includes important essays from Latin American scholars working in Spanish (like

Jorge Dubatti or Beatriz J. Rizk) and Latina/o theatre creators (like Gustavo Ott, Josefina Báez, and Astrid Hadad).

This type of cacophony that all those interactions can create is sustained in a thin balance by the curation and organization of the collection made by the editors. The way this collection is organized responds to a particular type of translation and adaptation—not through the means of converting texts formerly in Spanish into English—but of the ideas, approaches, and claims. Thus, the discourse that comes out of this collection and the frequent questions this study can raise in classrooms and conferences is remarkable.

There are some essential contributions this collection presents in the study of theatre and performance in general, and Latin America in particular, since they create a frame of reference for audiences in the United States to understand the Latin American artistic phenomena. Concepts as Jorge Dubatti's "teatro-matriz," or Josefina Báez' "performance autology;" ideas like Diego La Hoz' "Perú is an ambiguous country by nature. Perú is queer," or Claudio Valdés Kuri's "The terms 'Third World' and 'First World' correspond to economic denominations, to which art cannot circumscribe;" and arguments as Gustavo Ott's questioning "the traditional role of the author in the face of the globalized and mediatized world," or Ana Correa's necessity "to explore new possibilities of corporeal expression and theatrical staging" as a response to state-sponsored violence.

As an anthology about new discourses and new perspectives of the theatre and performance in and from Latin America, it is poised to become a foundational work in regards of the study of the region as a generator of different approaches to the theatrical phenomena, in an historiographic and a contemporary spectrum. In the Introduction, the editors mention about the collection that is an "effort to complicate and (re)envision the spaces and significances of Latin American and Latina/o performance practices from scholarly and artistic viewpoints," but this work goes beyond that, raising multiple questions and the strong desire to go deeper and know more about the Latina/o influence in the power structures from their theatre creations and performance traditions.

CARLOS SALAZAR Z.
University of Washington

INFORMATION FOR AUTHORS

Texas Theatre Journal invites manuscripts on a variety of topics related to theatre and the performing arts, with emphases on history, practice, criticism, and theory. In addition to full-length articles, *TTJ* publishes profiles, interviews, book reviews, and performance reviews.

While we proudly feature material about theatre and performance from throughout the Americas, the journal is particularly interested in research related to the broad geographical, cultural, and historical notion of Texas and the American Southwest. Published annually by the Texas Educational Theatre Association, we welcome opportunities to support scholars working in Texas, and our mandate is to feature the work of graduate students whenever possible.

Articles

We value clear, accessible writing for a general audience of theatre educators, scholars, and practitioners. Preferred articles are typically 4000-6000 words in length. Articles should be submitted via email as Word files, following Chicago Style guidelines with all citations/context notes handled as end notes. Accompanying photographs are welcome (author must secure permissions).

The article itself should be a reader's copy without author's name or affiliation; submissions should also include a title page with author(s) and affiliated institutions, along with an abstract of 500 words or less. Special consideration is given to articles with subject matter connected with or related to Texas, its border states, and/or the American Southwest. Articles will go through a thorough double-anonymous peer review process, and authors may be requested to make edits before publication.

Submissions should be emailed to the editors at TexasTheatreJournal@gmail.com.

Profiles and Interviews

Texas Theatre Journal publishes scholarly profiles and rigorous interviews covering theatre practitioners with a Texas connection. Accompanying photos are preferred (author must secure photo permissions). Article, Profile, and Interview submissions should be e-mailed to the editors at TexasTheatreJournal@gmail.com.

Performance and Book Reviews

Texas Theatre Journal invites book and performance reviews. Typical length is 800 words. Please contact the respective editors directly:

Performance Review Editor: Suzanne Delle (sdelle@ycp.edu);

Book Review Editor: Cason Murphy (cwmurphy@iastate.edu).

TETA Academic Symposium Scholars Debut Papers Panel

The purpose of the Academic Symposium is to provide a forum at the annual Theatrefest for scholars, teachers, students, professionals, and others interested in the scholarly inquiry of theatre-related topics. Attendees gather to present papers and discuss the ideas set forth as a group, thus creating an opportunity to share ideas and promote scholarship in the academic and professional theatre community.

The Academic Symposium theme changes yearly and can and should be interpreted broadly. Special consideration is given to papers with a focus on each year's theme; however, consideration is given to all proposals of theatre-related topics. Proposals for the Academic Symposium should include:

- Name
- School or Organization Affiliation
- Email address
- Title of the paper
- 150-250 word abstract
- A brief bio

As part of the Academic Symposium, the Scholars Debut Papers Panel (SDPP), provides a forum for young scholars (debut presenters – both undergraduate & graduate level) interested in the scholarly inquiry of theatre-related topics. Students submit short, clearly written papers concerned with any topic within the area of theatre or performance studies. Essay subjects require either systematic research, thoroughly documented in the paper, or the application, development, and/or creation of new theory or criticism. Students receive categorized feedback regarding their submission from anonymous theatre scholar reviewers. Selected winners (up to 3) are invited to TheatreFest to present their papers and discuss their ideas within a supportive scholarly group comprised of academics and theatre professionals. Additionally, awardees' papers are published in the next volume of *Texas Theatre Journal*. Student Guidelines for the Scholars Debut Papers Panel are:

- The subject of the essay should be one that requires either systematic research, thoroughly documented in the paper, or the application, development, and/or creation of new theory or criticism.
- The enrolled student must have written all submitted papers during the previous school year.
- The paper may not have been previously presented at a state, regional, or national conference, convention, or symposium. Papers which have been previously published or accepted for publication may not be submitted.
- Jointly written papers are not accepted.
- The title page must include the author's name, mailing address, telephone number(s), and email address in the lower right-hand corner.
- The title page should be followed by a second page with a biography of the author, one page or less in length.
- The essay itself should begin on the third page and be long enough to be read in approximately 15 minutes (8-12 pages.)
- Each student entering the competition must become a member of TETA; student membership is $20. This $20 payment and a completed copy of the membership registration form must accompany all submissions

The call for papers for both the Academic Symposium and the Scholars Debut Papers Panel are distributed in February of each year; the submission deadline is in April. All submission materials should be emailed in Word format to the Academic Symposium Coordinator, Prof. Rebecca Worley - rebecca.worley@tamuc.edu.

TETA Academic Symposium and Scholars Debut Papers Panel Committee:

Rebecca Worley,   Coordinator
Texas A&M University Commerce

Jackie Rosenfeld   Assistant Coordinator
Stephen F. Austin State University

Eric Skiles   Scholars Debut Papers/
Lone Star College-Kingwood   TETA Liaison

Note: The editors of TTJ reserve the right to request winners format their paper according to Chicago citation standards before being printed in Texas Theatre Journal, though this is <u>not</u> a requirement for submission to the Scholars Debut Papers Panel and may be delayed until after the conference.

ABOUT THE TEXAS EDUCATIONAL THEATRE ASSOCIATION

The Texas Educational Theatre Association strives to use all available resources to strengthen the quality of theatre education in the state of Texas. Since its founding in 1951, the Texas Educational Theatre Association, Inc. and its Committee on Academic and Production Standards have sought constantly to improve the status of drama and its teaching in Texas public schools and colleges. Membership in the Texas Educational Theatre Association is open to all who work or teach in the non-commercial theatre of Texas.

More information about the association, membership, and its many programs may be found at tetatx.com

 We are proud to feature the Armadillo—the State Small Mammal of Texas—as the official mascot of the *Texas Theatre Journal*.